TW & PF PEGRAM

UNDERSTANDING HIEROGLYPHS

UNDERSTANDING HIEROGLYPHS

A Quick and Simple Guide

HILARY WILSON

 MICHAEL O'MARA BOOKS LIMITED

First published in Great Britain in 1993 by
Michael O'Mara Books Limited
9 Lion Yard
Tremadoc Road
London SW4 7NQ

A CIP catalogue record for this book is
available from the British Library

ISBN 1–85479–164–8

Printed and bound by Butler and Tanner Ltd,
Frome and London.

CONTENTS

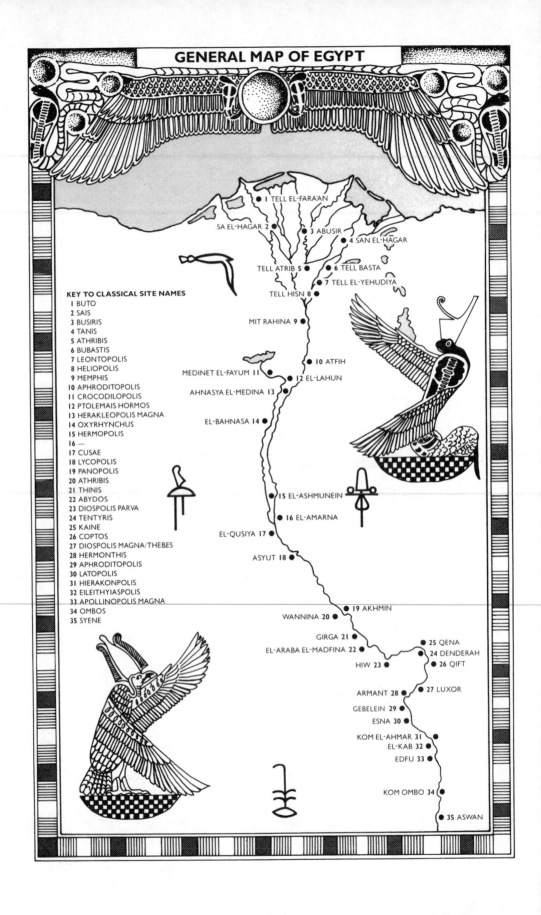

GENERAL MAP OF EGYPT

1 TELL EL-FARA'AN

SA EL-HAGAR 2   3 ABUSIR

4 SAN EL-HAGAR

TELL ATRIB 5   6 TELL BASTA

7 TELL EL-YEHUDIYA

TELL HISN 8

MIT RAHINA 9

KEY TO CLASSICAL SITE NAMES

1 BUTO
2 SAIS
3 BUSIRIS
4 TANIS
5 ATHRIBIS
6 BUBASTIS
7 LEONTOPOLIS
8 HELIOPOLIS
9 MEMPHIS
10 APHRODITOPOLIS
11 CROCODILOPOLIS
12 PTOLEMAIS HORMOS
13 HERAKLEOPOLIS MAGNA
14 OXYRHYNCHUS
15 HERMOPOLIS
16 —
17 CUSAE
18 LYCOPOLIS
19 PANOPOLIS
20 ATHRIBIS
21 THINIS
22 ABYDOS
23 DIOSPOLIS PARVA
24 TENTYRIS
25 KAINE
26 COPTOS
27 DIOSPOLIS MAGNA/THEBES
28 HERMONTHIS
29 APHRODITOPOLIS
30 LATOPOLIS
31 HIERAKONPOLIS
32 EILEITHYIASPOLIS
33 APOLLINOPOLIS MAGNA
34 OMBOS
35 SYENE

10 ATFIH

MEDINET EL-FAYUM 11   12 EL-LAHUN

AHNASYA EL-MEDINA 13

EL-BAHNASA 14

15 EL-ASHMUNEIN

16 EL-AMARNA

EL-QUSIYA 17

ASYUT 18

19 AKHMIN

WANNINA 20

GIRGA 21   25 QENA

EL-ARABA EL-MADFINA 22   24 DENDERAH

HIW 23   26 QIFT

ARMANT 28   27 LUXOR

GEBELEIN 29

ESNA 30

KOM EL-AHMAR 31

EL-KAB 32

EDFU 33

KOM OMBO 34

35 ASWAN

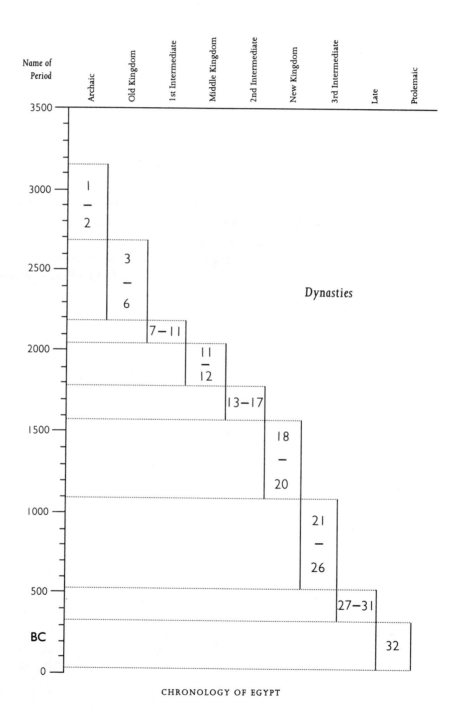

Name of
Period

Archaic

Old Kingdom

1st Intermediate

Middle Kingdom

2nd Intermediate

New Kingdom

3rd Intermediate

Late

Ptolemaic

Dynasties

3500

3000
1
–
2

2500
3
–
6

7–11

2000
11
–
12

13–17

1500
18
–
20

1000
21
–
26

500
27–31

BC
32

0

CHRONOLOGY OF EGYPT

ACKNOWLEDGMENTS

This book develops the theme of a day school entitled 'Name, Rank and Number in Ancient Egypt', which was held in May 1992 in Southampton. It has come into being as a result of the encouragement and enthusiasm of my students, and the support and understanding of my family.

The line drawings are all my own work; the maps were designed and drawn by Peter Funnell, a friend and fellow Egyptomane, who is also responsible for the jacket photographs.

INTRODUCTION

The latest-dated Egyptian hieroglyphs were carved at the Philae Temple in AD 394. By that late date there could have been relatively few Egyptian sculptors who could read, much less understand, the signs they were commissioned to carve. From the death of Alexander the Great in 323 BC until the Roman conquest in 30 BC Egypt was ruled by a family of Macedonian Greeks, the Ptolemies, and during that period Greek became the official court language. Important decrees were made bilingual and the Egyptian demotic script, called by the scribes the 'writing of the documents', superseded the more ancient hieratic script and was used even for carving inscriptions in stone. Hieroglyphs, which were known as the 'Words of the God', were still used for monumental inscriptions, particularly on the magnificent temples built by the Ptolemies in an attempt to gain the approval of the Egyptians and their gods. None the less signs were often chosen for their decorative effect rather than according to Egyptian scribal tradition. Some signs changed in meaning or sound and mistakes were commonly made in transferring the scribe's original text on to the carved or painted surface.

As Latin became the diplomatic language of the Western world and Egypt was finally absorbed into the Roman Empire, sizeable immigrant communities of Greeks and Romans were established in the country, especially in the lush, agricultural lands of the north. The native language was still spoken, of course, by the ordinary Egyptians who came to be known as Copts, a name originating in the Greek word for Egypt, *Aiguptos*, but since they were largely illiterate, the written language rapidly declined. The immigrants, unable to cope with the intricacies of any of the Egyptian scripts, adopted a written version of the language which is now called Coptic. This is the ancient Egyptian language in its latest, most decadent form, transcribed into the Greek alphabet with the addition of seven extra letters, ultimately derived from hieroglyphs, which were needed to express sounds not found in Greek.

In the last centuries of its use, the hieroglyphic script was used less and less by fewer and fewer scribes whose skills became ever weaker. Important scholastic works, notably the history of Egypt written by the Egyptian priest Manetho around the third century BC, were composed in Greek. In the third century AD another Egyptian priest, with the Greco-Egyptian name Hor-Apollo, wrote a book in Coptic which had a dramatic effect on the study of Egyptian hieroglyphs for many hundreds of years. Hor-Apollo's work consisted of a list of hieroglyphs together with their interpretations, but it is clear from his insistence that each sign had a single pictorial or symbolic meaning that he completely misunderstood the writing system used by his ancestors. Unfortunately, because it was considered to have been written by someone informed, Hor-Apollo's work was used as a guide for all future students of hieroglyphs.

The Coptic language survived the Arab conquest of Egypt in AD 639–42, principally because it had been adopted for the liturgy of the Egyptian Christian Church. In 1643 Father Athanasius Kircher was the first European scholar to identify Coptic as the last remnants of the popular tongue of the ancient Egyptians. His theories did not meet with universal acceptance and his attempts to translate hieroglyphic inscriptions were wildly conjectural, not to say absurd. However Kircher's recognition of the importance of Coptic to the deciphering of hieroglyphs led to his publishing a Coptic dictionary and grammar which became essential tools for all would-be students of Egyptology. One such student was Jean-François Champollion who was eventually to decipher the hieroglyphic script, publishing his *Précis du Système hieroglyphique* in 1823.

Thus for more than 1500 years the hieroglyphic script remained unreadable. Considering its beauty and its use on obviously religious buildings such as the great temples which had attracted European tourists for several centuries, it is hardly surprising that people should have thought that many esoteric secrets were concealed within its marvellous imagery. Egypt was seen as a source of mystery and magic, so much so that even the Romany people of Europe, viewed with great suspicion by the English in medieval times, were called Egyptians, shortened to gypsies. The association of mystery with all things Egyptian is also found in alchemy, the pseudo-scientific search for the Philosopher's Stone, which would give its possessor the power to transmute base metals into gold. This term derives from the Arabic expression 'that of Kem', Kem being one of the ancient names for Egypt. Thus the more legitimate descendant of alchemy, the science of chemistry, also owes its name, though not its origins, to ancient Egypt.

The search for the key to the understanding of the hieroglyphic script was undertaken for a variety of reasons. Some philosophers hoped to find ancient wisdom and long-forgotten truths. Religious scholars wished to find confirmation of biblical stories and proof of the existence of such figures as Abraham, Joseph and Moses. More self-interested students believed that the decipherment of the script would lead to fabulous wealth as the secrets of the Pharaohs' treasures were revealed. Only the true academics saw the decipherment of the script as an end in itself, thus only the true academics were not disappointed. Hieroglyphs may be highly decorative but they are no more than a means of writing down words. Those words may be philosophical, or historical, or religious but more often than not they are straightforward, mundane and repetitive.

The great museums of the world house many magnificent Egyptian works of art, including sculpture, reliefs and paintings, which are lavishly inscribed with hieroglyphs. Once the signs could be translated it was found that the words and phrases which occurred most often were names and titles, often of gods or kings, and simple formulas and prayers. Even in the grandest monuments, like the Karnak Temple and the tombs in the Valley of Kings, the inscriptions are found to include the names and epithets of kings and gods repeated ad nauseam. Names, titles and expressions including numbers, such as dates, are among the most easily recognizable of hieroglyphic terms and, forming as they do a large proportion of the accessible inscriptions, they provide an ideal area in which the keen amateur may practise some basic skills in reading ancient Egyptian. Having some background information about the cultural and social significance of such terms turns a simple reading exercise into a lesson in appreciation of the society that created them.

Key to reading Hieroglyphs

Egyptian hieroglyphs were written in rows or columns which could be read from left to right or from right to left. In order to identify the direction in which a particular text is to be read it is necessary only to look at the human or animal figures which always face towards the beginning of the line or series of columns. Having identified where the inscription starts the second rule to follow is that upper is read before lower. This means that columns are always read from top to bottom and, in groups of hieroglyphs which have been arranged to fill a space neatly, the upper signs are read first, always observing the direction dictated by the orientation of the figures. Examples of the ways in which a text may be written are shown in figure 1 (opposite), with the numbers indicating the order in which the signs are to be read. The order of reading the signs is not altered by the change in the direction of the inscription, so the sign marked 3 is always the third sign in the text.

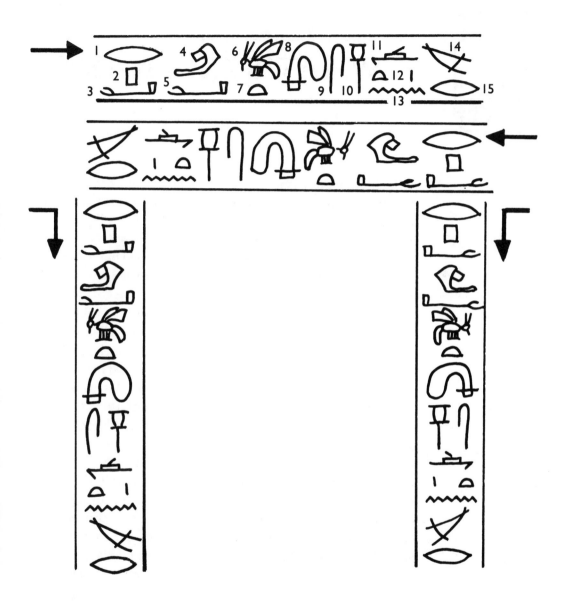

Figure 1

1. WHAT'S IN A NAME?

At the head of this chapter are to be found the twin cartouches of the best-known of all Egyptian kings – Tutankhamen. 'Cartouche' is not itself an Egyptian word but is the French for cartridge. The oval shape, in the form of a loop of rope, which enclosed the names of the king, was seen to resemble the sausage-shaped bundle of powder and shot with which eighteenth-century French artillery-men loaded their guns.

Identifying Tutankhamen's names on monuments established that he had existed, while Theodore Davies's discovery in 1908 of the same names inscribed on some of the remains of the king's funerary banquet, suggested that he had been buried in or around the Valley of Kings. Howard Carter, convinced by this evidence that there was a tomb to be found, determined to unearth it, finally making his greatest discovery in 1922. All this was achieved despite the fact that Tutankhamen had been officially forgotten, effectively becoming a non-person when his name was expunged by his successors from the contemporary record very shortly after his death. The modern resurrection of his name has led, by Egyptian standards, to immortality for Tutankhamen. The fact that we speak his name, no matter how badly we might pronounce it, means that he is remembered. This was considered essential if his spirit was to survive into the next, eternal life. As his name lives, so does he.

In ancient Egypt a person's name was not just an identifying label, it was part of that person's very being, and as such was far more important than names are in our modern, Western society. Know-ledge of the true names of things gave power over those things. According to Egyptian myth, the god Re-Atum had only to conceive a thing in his mind and speak its name for it to come into being. Thus, as he had given everything a name at its creation, he alone had power over all things. This same idea is expressed in Genesis 2: 19–20, in which God is described as giving Adam the power of naming all the animals of creation so that man might have dominion over beasts:

> And out of the ground the Lord God formed every beast of the field and every fowl of the air; and brought them unto Adam to see what he would call them; and whatsoever Adam called every living creature, that was the name thereof. And Adam gave names to all cattle, and to the fowl of the air and to every beast of the field.

Some primitive societies still maintain the superstition of not revealing one's real name except to the tribal chief and, maybe, to one's closest family. In ancient Egypt it was believed that even Re himself had a secret name which he alone knew. A story preserved in a Nineteenth-Dynasty papyrus in the Turin Museum tells how the goddess Isis sought to obtain Re's secret name. It was said that as he wandered about the earth Re appeared as an aged man, his limbs enfeebled, his back stooped, his head shaking and his mouth drooling like an infant. Seeing this, Isis watched where the god passed and noted where his spittle fell to the ground. She took up the mud formed from the dry earth and the god's saliva and moulded it into a serpent which she then caused to come alive – not for nothing was Isis known as the Mistress of Magic. Having been made from what issued from Re's mouth the snake was a true creation but as Re had not named it he had no power over it. Only Isis knew the serpent's name. She left the snake in Re's path so that when next he walked that way it bit the god's heel. Feeling the poison coursing through his limbs like fire, Re called on every venomous beast that he had created, ordering it to take away the pain, but he could not call upon the true culprit for he had not controlled its creation. Eventually he called upon Isis who had a reputation as a healer and was the acknowledged expert in dealing with bites and stings. She said she would cure Re but only on the condition that he would reveal to her his true name. He tried to bluff her by reciting several of his lesser-known names but Isis was not to be fooled so easily. The pain grew and Re was in such agony that at last he agreed to give away the most powerful secret of all. Even then Isis drove a hard bargain and insisted that she should be allowed to reveal the name to her son Horus. In his delirium Re submitted. He told Isis the name and the goddess summoned away the poison.

Isis is shown in many guises but this story demonstrates both her cunning and her devotion to her son in procuring for him the greatest gift of all, knowledge of the true name of Re. The story of the secret name of God is echoed in the Islamic fable concerning the one hundred names of Allah. It is said that all one hundred names were revealed to the Prophet who passed on ninety-nine of them to the faithful. The hundredth name he whispered to his camel which explains why the camel wears such a superior expression; after all, the camel knows something that mere humans do not and that something is a name of power.

Egyptian gods also had many names. Some religious texts include lengthy sections devoted to the naming of gods in their various aspects so that the appropriate form of a particular deity might be invoked for a specific purpose. The sun-god, for example, was known by many names, each seen as a different god. The supreme solar deity was Re (or Ra), the god of the sun at its height. He was commonly portrayed as a man with a falcon's head on which the sun's disc was worn as a crown. The creator Atum was also associated with the sun, often being named as Re-Atum. He was the sun in its descent from noon to sunset in the west and especially in the dangerous realms of the underworld through which it had to travel each night to reappear in the east at dawn the next day. He was portrayed as an elderly and, therefore, wise man. The sun at its rising and setting was Harakhty, meaning 'Horus of the Two Horizons', seen as a soaring or diving falcon. The sun-god who was seen to ascend through the morning sky was Khepri, the scarab beetle, pushing the sun before him as the insect rolls its ball of dung. The name Khepri derives from the verb 'to become' or 'to change' and has the same stem as the noun 'form' or 'shape'. Tutankhamen's coronation name may be translated as 'Many are the Forms of Re'. This might just as well be read 'Many are the Names of Re', for, as we have seen, the name was the essence of the form.

In the *Litany of Re*, a religious text one example of which is found in the tomb of Thutmose III, no fewer than seventy-five forms of Re are listed. One chapter of the funerary text known as the *Book of Amduat* (meaning 'that which is in the Underworld'), commonly called the *Book of the Dead*, deals exclusively with the names of Osiris as is indicated by its title, *Knowing the Names of Osiris in His Every Seat Where He Desires to Be*. This multiplicity of names or titles is neatly expressed in the opening lines of a Hymn to Osiris found on an Eighteenth-Dynasty stela now in the Louvre:

> Hail to you, Osiris,
> Lord of Eternity, king of gods,
> Of many names, of holy forms

The stanza goes on to list those names and 'holy forms'.

In naming deities it was very important to be precise: it would never do to insult a god by addressing him impolitely. In the journey between this world and the next, traversing the perilous paths of the underworld, the deceased needed to know many names. There were gates to be opened and waterways to cross, each with its own guardian or ferryman. Passage could be gained only by addressing each respectfully and by name. The demons and dangerous creatures of the darkness could be subdued or neutralized only if their names were known.

As part of the examination for entry into the realms of Osiris, the deceased had to make what is now called the 'Negative Confession' (fig.2). Rather than say what he had done wrong in his life he had to make a series of specific statements about what he had *not* done. Each statement had to be made before the correct deity who had to be given the correct name and epithet. There were forty-two judges requiring forty-two sets, each consisting of a statement, name and title to be remembered, so it is hardly surprising that a wise man should include in his tomb a written version of this 'Negative Confession' – an examination crib sheet! Once this had been successfully delivered the deceased went on to the 'Weighing of the Heart', a scene commonly shown on the walls of New Kingdom tombs and in papyrus versions of the *Book of the Dead*. If he had not told the truth or had not lived as blameless a life as he claimed, his

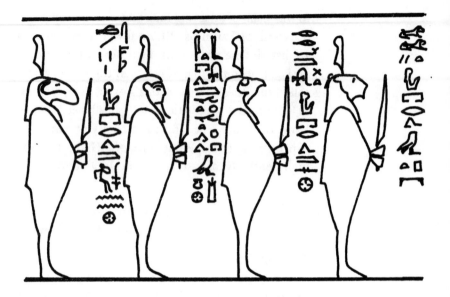

2. Four of the forty-two assessor-gods to whom the 'Negative Confession' was made. In front of each figure is the name and epithet by which the deceased must address the deity.

Translation (from right to left):
1. Twin-Lions, who comes from heaven [The eastern and western horizons were seen to rest on the backs of two lions.]
2. He of the Burning Eyes, who comes from Sa [Sais?]
3. The Fiery One who comes forth backwards out of Iunu [Heliopolis]
4. The Breaker of Bones, who comes from Nesen [Herakleopolis]

heart would weigh heavier than the feather of truth and he would be denied everlasting life. If the 'Weighing of the Heart' was satisfactory, he would be proclaimed 'True of Voice' or 'Justified', meaning that his confession had not been false, and that he had justified his claim to eternal life.

The rituals just described required, of course, the deceased to have a voice. The power of speech, together with the other senses, was restored to the body by a ritual known as 'Opening the Mouth'. This was traditionally one of the last acts in the funeral rites and included the application of various oils and ointments to the mask covering the head of the mummified body, or to the anthropomorphic coffin, or even to a portrait statue of the deceased. Speech was restored by touching the mouth with an instrument similar to a woodworker's adze. This act was usually performed by the eldest son of the family who thus earned the title 'He who Causes their Names to Live' (fig.3). It was his duty to see to the funeral preparations and ritual, the filling and sealing of the tomb and the maintenance of mortuary rites and offerings to continue the memory and, thus, the existence of his parents.

A prudent man would make as much provision for the survival of his name as he could possibly afford. A stela was usually erected before the tomb, in the tomb chapel or set into the tomb wall. This recorded the names and titles of the tomb-owner and his immediate family. The names would be repeated many times within the tomb itself, in paintings and reliefs, on statues and in documents such as funerary papyri, all ensuring the survival of the identity of the owner. Pottery cones, thought to be imitation offering loaves, were often arranged as a frieze above the tomb entrance, their round bases turned outwards to reveal the impressed names and titles of the person buried within. Boxes, baskets and shrines were all sealed by means of twisted cords, the knots embedded in a lump of clay which was impressed while damp with a seal of ownership. Jars had their lids sealed on with clay which could also be impressed with a scarab seal while the shoulders of the jars could be marked directly in ink. The owner's name was everywhere, even in laundry marks on bed linen.

3. Part of a text from a funerary stela describing the son of the tomb owners.
Translation: Their beloved son, who causes their names to live, the King's Acquaintance, his true and beloved.

A woman would usually share her husband's tomb as would any children who had died young or unmarried. The extended family included both the living and the dead who were often portrayed as adults even when they had died as infants. Although the memory of a name was enough to confer immortality, names recorded in their written forms or spoken by priests or well-wishers were considered to be more secure than trusting to the fickle memories of one's family. Egyptian society was based on family life and the people

fervently hoped that all the members of their families would be reunited after death. So it was essential that the necessary rituals were carried out by the surviving relatives who, in their turn, would receive the same duty from their heirs. No one wished to face great-grandpa in the next world and have to explain why his mortuary offerings had been allowed to lapse. A more affluent family would set up an endowment in the form of a tract of land whose revenues provided for the employment of professional mortuary priests. These priests carried out the rituals and made the offerings or, at the very least, recited the names of the deceased as listed on the tomb stela. It was, of course, greatly preferable for these duties to be carried out by one who cared, usually the eldest or eldest surviving son. In the event that no son outlived his father, the nearest male relative – brother, grandson or even son-in-law – could act as the celebrant in the 'Opening of the Mouth' ritual. In Tutankhamen's case his successor Ay is shown performing this rite in the king's tomb. No child of the royal couple is known to have survived. In this case the relationship between the deceased and his heir is far from clear, but the fact of his performing this ceremony may well indicate that Ay was Tutankhamen's closest, living, male relative (fig.4).

Although there is no contemporary Egyptian reference to the Seven Plagues mentioned in the Bible, the threat of the death of the firstborn would have been much more of a blow to Egyptian

4. King Ay, as the heir of Tutankhamen, performs the 'Opening of the Mouth' ritual for the deceased king who is shown in the guise of Osiris. Ay wears the cheetah-skin robe of the *sem* priest, and the 'Blue War Crown', and has his names shown in cartouche.

Translation (above Tutankhamen, columns from right to left):
1. The Good God, Lord of the Two Lands, Lord of Appearances,
2. King of Upper and Lower Egypt, (Neb-kheperu-Re) given life,
3. Son of Re, (Tutankhamen, Ruler of Thebes) forever.
   (above Ay, columns from left to right)
1. The Good God, Lord of the Two Lands, Lord of Action,
2. King of Upper and Lower Egypt, (Kheper-kheperu-Re)
   [one scarab sign was omitted from the cartouche by the scribe]
3. Son of Re, (The Father of the God, Ay)
4. Given Life, like Re, forever and ever

society than it might appear. It not only promised to destroy a living generation, it also threatened to annihilate all those whose memory the sons would have been expected to perpetuate. Such a plague would strike the dead as well as the living. The importance of the son's role is also apparent in the Babylonian language where the words for 'son' and 'name' are identical.

The Egyptians hoped that everything they had enjoyed in their mortal existence would be available to them in the next life. Food, drink, furniture, clothing – indeed all the creature comforts – could be provided for the afterlife in several ways. Real items could be included among the burial goods, either prepared especially for the tomb or taken from the owner's earthly possessions, but models of the same things, such as wooden loaves of bread, or carved stone fruit, would do just as well. They could be made real by the know-ledge of their names. Paintings or reliefs could give even more detail and be longer lasting. For example, a scene showing the harvest of grain would ensure that, should the offerings lapse or the tomb stocks run low, the tomb-owner could be provided with bread and beer from the produce of the painted fields. Indeed, scenes of the harvested grain being turned into bread and beer made the provision even more certain. As long as the scenes lasted they could be activated by means of words, giving each element its correct name, describing each action concisely and precisely.

It has to be said that no well-to-do Egyptian would have liked the idea of having to put his shoulder to the plough or wield a sickle. In life he would have had servants to perform such tasks, so in death he took his servants with him – not in body but in effigy. The custom of a king's servants being sacrificed at his death to be buried with him is only attested for a very short period at the beginning of dynastic history. Such a wasteful practice was soon superseded by the inclusion of tomb paintings and reliefs or models showing such household chores as baking, weaving and woodworking, together with the necessary servants to carry out these menial but essential tasks. On occasion the servants were themselves named, thus being assured a little immortality in their own right. In the later periods, elaborate three-dimensional models were replaced by simple servant figures called *shabtis* who were sometimes provided with miniature tools and coffins or storage boxes of their own. A *shabti* was a jack-of-all-trades and in most examples of the 'Book of the Dead' the correct *shabti* inscription is included. This is supposed to be a statement by the *shabti* to the effect that, should his master, the tomb-owner, require any work to be done in the next world, or should he be summoned to do any work in the realm of Osiris by the god himself, then at the mention of his name the *shabti* will stand forward saying, 'Here am I', answering in his master's place. *Shabti* means 'answerer'. The majority of *shabtis* have a very brief inscription which is almost meaningless in many cases. These little figures were, by Egyptian standards, mass-produced and were presented by mourners at a funeral in rather the same way as wreaths are given at modern, Western funerals. However bastard-ized the inscription, the purpose of the *shabtis* was always the same. They were intended to be activated in response to their master's name. The name was a powerful thing for it could mobilize a workforce of unquestioning loyalty and untiring effort.

A man's name was vulnerable in ways other than being simply forgotten. Paintings and reliefs could be chiselled from walls, statues could be broken and their inscriptions defaced. The name and thus the immortal existence of a person could be destroyed utterly by a determined enemy, so the more times the name was repeated the harder that enemy's task became. There are several well-known examples of attempts to destroy a person by such means. The tomb of Rekhmire, Vizier during the reigns of Amenhotep II and Thutmose IV, was systematically attacked. His portrait, name and titles were cut from the walls, though not thoroughly enough to hide his identity. It is impossible to say who was responsible for this act of vandalism or why it was done. It is not unlikely that Rekhmire, holding as he did the most important administrative position in the land, had made enemies. Alternatively, he could have fallen from grace and the desecration of his tomb could then have been an officially sanctioned act.

The tomb of the architect Senenmut, one of the chief ministers at the court of Queen Hatshepsut, and tutor to her daughter Princess Neferure, suffered a similar fate but his enemies went even further in demonstrating their hatred. They also attacked the tombs of his parents and other members of his family. This almost fanatical destruction of these monuments was still not enough to obscure the names of the tomb owners. They are remembered while the names of their desecrators are totally forgotten.

A more successful attack was made on another of Hatshepsut's officials who had been responsible for quarrying and erecting a pair of obelisks, one of which still stands at Karnak. In his tomb some inscriptions remain from which it is possible to identify him as the overseer of this work and to read the list of titles which he held, but his name is nowhere to be seen. Nor was royalty immune from such displays of spite or revenge. The monuments of Hatshepsut herself were treated to similar desecration by her successor and erstwhile co-regent Thutmose III. Reliefs on the topmost parts of the obelisks which she presented to Amen at the Karnak Temple showed her receiving the god's blessing. Thutmose had the names and figure of his mother-in-law chiselled out of the granite and replaced by a pair of innocuous offering-tables laden with flowers.

There are instances of names being replaced by other names. In the Memphite tomb of Horemheb one of his closest servants, Sementawy, is shown on several occasions accompanying his master at official functions. It seems that Sementawy died before the tomb was completed for his name was overcut with that of Ramose who took over his duties in Horemheb's household. At Akhetaten, now known as Amarna, the city built by Akhenaten, the names of his wives, Nefertiti and Kia, are sometimes replaced by those of his eldest daughter, Meritaten. This could be an indication of either death or disgrace, most probably the former. Such alterations can be a help to archaeologists in dating a monument or putting the complexities of Egyptian history into some sort of order.

It was also during the reign of Akhenaten that another form of name-desecration took place; this time the victims were gods. Akhenaten had introduced the very exclusive cult of the Aten, yet another solar deity being the physical aspect of the sun itself, the sun's disc. In the latter part of his reign he ordered workmen to remove the names of all gods other than the Aten and the supreme deity Re from all monuments. Thebes, the city of Amen who was considered to be the Aten's greatest rival, suffered most from this

5. From the top section of Hatshepsut's obelisk, now lying in the first court at Karnak. The Queen is shown receiving the blessing of Amen whose figure and titles had been erased on the orders of Akhenaten then recut at a later date. The dotted lines show the extent of the damage.

Translation (columns read from left to right):
1. To be said by Amen-Re, Lord of Heaven 'May there be given to . . .
2. 'She of the "Two Lands", complete authority', to the Daughter [of Re]
3. [Maet-ka-Re], likewise love, that she may live

iconoclasm and even the name of the king's father, Amenhotep III, had the Amen element defaced. On another of Hatshepsut's obelisks it is still possible to see where the figure of Amen and his name were removed from the original relief only to be recut at a later date when other kings tried to atone for Akhenaten's blasphemy (fig.5).

In an attempt to restore themselves to the favour of the gods, later kings denied Akhenaten's very existence by omitting his name, and those of his three short-lived successors, from official lists.

Horemheb even dated his reign from the death of Amenhotep III. Although this constituted a less than total destruction of their memory, the official namelessness of these monarchs was a clear message to all that they were *personae non gratae*.

Other people who were considered enemies, either national or personal, were the subject of what are now termed 'Execration Texts'. These were short texts vilifying individuals, foreigners or even general evils such as disease, any of which might pose a severe threat to a tomb-owner. They were inscribed on stone flakes or rough, unglazed pottery which were then deliberately smashed and buried outside the tomb. It was as if the writing of the name trapped the essential being in the substance of the pot so that when it was broken the named enemy was destroyed, or at least disabled. The ceremony of breaking the red pots shown in Horemheb's Memphite tomb is thought to refer to this execration ritual (fig.6).

6. A mourner, shown in the Memphite tomb of Horemheb, wailing over the 'Breaking of the Red Pots', a ritual associated with the 'Execration Texts'.

The king's enemies were portrayed as captives with their arms bound behind them at the elbow. In lists of the king's victories in battle each conquered foe has his body replaced by a cartouche-like oval containing the name of the defeated. This had the same

 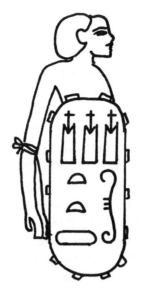 

7. Three of the 'Nine Bows' from the Theban tomb of Surer, shown as bound captives with their bodies replaced by walled cartouches.

Translation (from right to left):
1. The Libyans
2. The tribes of Nubia
3. Those dwelling in Asia

purpose as the 'Execration Texts'. The portrayal of the bound captives, named and differentiated by racial characteristics such as skin colour and hairstyle, was a way of putting those particular foes at the mercy of the king. Bound captives, with or without the cartouche-body, were often used as decorative elements in relief, for example around the bases of the colossal statues of Ramesses II at Abu Simbel or on the dais upon which Amenhotep III and Queen Tiye are shown enthroned in the tomb of Kheruef. Lists of the campaign victories of Thutmose III are displayed in the same form at Karnak (fig.7).

The seal of the Royal Necropolis which was used to impress the plaster or clay sealings on the doors of the tombs in the 'Valley of Kings' showed nine bound captives, representing the traditional enemies of Egypt, surmounted by the jackal-god Anubis. This god was seen as the Guardian of the Necropolis and in the image on the seal he holds captive all the enemies of the king. Set at the very entrance to the tomb, this seal served the same purpose as the 'Execration Texts' (see fig.9, page 29).

Another important catalogue of names is the King List. In several monuments, notably the Temple of Seti I at Abydos, lists of the reigning monarch's predecessors are set out on the walls, accompanied by a scene of the king and his eldest son paying homage to their ancestors. Each ruler needed only to be represented by his cartouche for the name *was* the person. These King Lists are very useful to Egyptologists even though they are not always complete. The Amarna kings are usually omitted as can be seen in the Abydos King List of Ramesses II in the British Museum, and those whose reigns were short or undistinguished were not thought worthy of being remembered. As these are monuments to the kings who commissioned them, the names of their authors are likely to occur more often than that of any of their illustrious forebears. The outward display of regality and power required, almost by definition, the prominent use of names and titles. A monument to the glory of Ramesses II, for example, would be unthinkable without the deeply incised decorative use of his cartouches (fig.8).

8. The cartouches of Ramesses II, giving his official and personal names. The first is the origin of Ozymandias in Shelley's poem of that name.

Translation:
Left: King of Upper & Lower Egypt, (User-Maet-Re, Setep-en-Re)
Right: Son of Re, (Ramesses Mi-Amen)

An Egyptian statue was not considered to be a work of art but was a substitute for the real person, serving a very real purpose. The features were, more often than not, conventionalized so that few statues can be said with confidence to be life-portraits, but as long as each was duly inscribed with the name of its owner it was considered to be a true likeness. The name made it real. A *ka* or spirit-statue was included in tombs as an alternative abode for the *ka* or spiritual part of the deceased's personality. These statues show more realism than some of the official royal and religious statues in temples, but all have one thing in common. Without a naming inscription either on the statue or nearby, a statue represented no one. Without a name an ancient Egyptian did not exist. The possibility of losing one's name and therefore one's very existence was a very real fear, so much so that a prayer for remembrance was included in the 'Book of the Dead':

Spell for causing the deceased to be remembered in the realm of the dead.

A name has been given to me in the shrines of Upper Egypt, my name has been remembered in the shrines of Lower Egypt, on that night of reckoning the years and of counting the months. . . . As for any god who shall not come following after me, I shall declare his name to those who are yet to be.

Figure 9

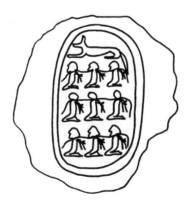

2. PERSONAL NAMES

Egyptian was an unpointed language, as are printed Arabic and Hebrew, meaning they are written without vowels. Figure 10 (opposite) shows the hieroglyphic signs now recognized as being alphabetic. Approximate sound-values have been given for each of the signs, which include some semi-vowels or weak consonants like the *alif* and *ayin* of Arabic, both of which may be pronounced as 'ah'. In cases where vowels are necessary to pronunciation the modern convention is to insert the letter 'e', so that the word for 'name', which is spelled 'rn', is usually pronounced 'ren'. This does not mean that this is how the word was spoken, it is simply a convenient aid to students of ancient Egyptian. Neither does it indicate that 'e' was the most common vowel sound in the ancient tongue. This practice is no more than a recently accepted means of vocalizing the language. In fact there are very few clues as to how the language sounded, so modern pronunciation is largely a matter of educated guesswork and the source of much learned discussion, not to say argument.

The hieroglyphic 'alphabet' is conventionally arranged according to the order of a Semitic alphabet like Arabic. The last four signs in the centre of the last row of the alphabet chart are commonly used alternatives for signs already listed. See below for the use of the last sign, the lion hieroglyph. The mouth-sign 'r' was also used occasionally in place of 'l'.

When the Rosetta Stone was found in 1799, French scholars quickly realized how important a discovery it was, for the text inscribed upon it was repeated in three different scripts – hieroglyphic, demotic and Greek. Since the last was a known language it could be used to decipher the Egyptian inscriptions. The British physicist Thomas Young made some headway in identifying words

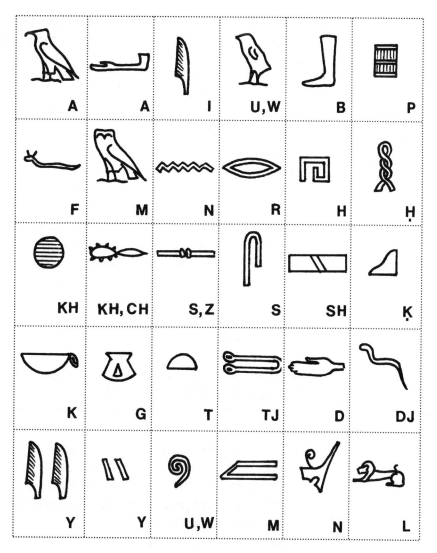

Figure 10

within the demotic text and made the important observation that there seemed to be phonetic elements within the script. His Egyptian studies were no more than a holiday diversion, a relaxing interlude in his more important work, but his observations were valid and almost certainly came to the notice of Champollion who was working on the same texts in France.

Champollion concentrated on the hieroglyphic inscription and was the first to realize that there were far too few individual hieroglyphs for the script to be purely pictorial and yet too many for it to be entirely phonetic. He also noticed that the positions of names within the Greek text could correspond with those oval cartouches which clearly marked out important words or phrases in the hieroglyphic section. It was, therefore, the names in the Rosetta Stone inscription which gave the clue to the decipherment of the hieroglyphic script as a whole.

The values assigned by Champollion to the hieroglyphs in the names Ptolemy and Cleopatra were based on the correct assumption that, being of foreign origin, (Macedonian Greek), they would have had no meaning in the Egyptian language and would have had to be spelled out phonetically (see fig. 11). Thus he identified some signs as vowels which, in the light of later studies, have been shown to be weak consonants or bi-literal signs. The 'o' in both Ptolemy and Cleopatra is indicated by a looped rope or lasso which has the phonetic value 'wa', and there are two different signs used where a 't' would be expected which indicates that one, now recognized as a 'd', was pronounced somewhat more softly than the other. The lion symbol, to which Champollion assigned the value 'l', was in fact an Egyptian compromise. As in Japanese, the sound 'l' does not occur in ancient Egyptian and the Egyptians had great difficulty in pronouncing this consonant. In foreign words or names the 'l' was usually replaced by 'r' or a compound 'rw', the latter being the phonetic value of the lion sign. Altogether this gives the impression that the Egyptians pronounced the names Ptwarwmys (Ptolemaios) and Krwiwapadra (Cleopatra).

This is one of the clues to the ancient pronunciation of the language. Further ideas can be gained from the writings of classical authors who Hellenized and Latinized Egyptian names to make life easier for their readers. This Hellenization could be said to have started with Herodotus who visited Egypt around 400 BC. He was the sort of tourist still adored by modern guides. He soaked up everything he was told and reported it in his *Histories* for readers to draw their own conclusions as to what was true and what was fantasy. The Egyptian priest Manetho also wrote in Greek and used

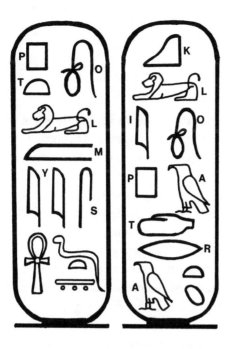

11. The cartouches of Ptolemy (left) and Cleopatra (right) showing how common sounds in the two names led to the identification of some alphabetic signs.

names which came more easily to Greek tongues. These Hellenized names are still in common use so the goddess Ast or Iset became Isis, and her husband Wsir is better known as Osiris. The kings Amenhotep are often called Amenophis and the city of Men-nefer is always referred to as Memphis. Although these have been changed from their Egyptian forms they are not so different as to completely hide the original pronunciation. The god Amen had his name written as Imn in Egyptian but the Romans worshipped him as Ammon, associating him with Jupiter. This gives a very good idea of how they heard the name and how it could be vocalized today. However the same god may have his name spelled out as Amen, Amon or Amun, the last being pronounced in recent years as Amoon. There seems to be no justification for the use of any one of these in preference to any other since the vowel between the 'm' and 'n' was not written in the hieroglyphic form. In this book the spelling preferred is Amen, continuing the use of the inserted 'e' for ease of pronunciation.

Because the Greeks and Romans tried to associate Egyptian gods with deities of the classical pantheon, or perhaps because they could not get their tongues around the original names, the names of some gods have become corrupted beyond recognition. The ibis-headed god of writing is known as Thoth which was altered by the Greeks from the Egyptian Djehuti (see fig.31, page 97). By modern convention the Greek version of this name is used in personal names but it may still occur in several different spellings. The royal name Thutmose may be written as Tuthmosis, Tuthmose, Thotmes or even Tahutimes. The last is, in fact, closest to the original pronunciation, as far as can be judged. Strangely, when the same name is given to a non-royal person it is usually transcribed as something even closer to the Egyptian – Djehutimes. It is also one of the names which could be used by both men and women without an ending to indicate gender.

Another corruption arose due to a misunderstanding. When Roman tourists asked which god was worshipped at the magnificent temple at Saqqara, beneath which are the burial vaults for the sacred Apis bulls of Memphis, they were told 'Wsir Api' meaning 'the dead Apis'. In other words, this was the mortuary temple where the cult of the dead bulls was celebrated. The Romans interpreted the reply as the name of a god calling him Serapis and the temple and burial complex is still known as the Serapeum. This deity became enormously popular and was worshipped in his own temple in Rome in the form of a man with a full shaggy beard, which was a most un-Egyptian feature, and nothing to do with a bull at all.

In hieroglyphs it was common to write certain signs or groups of signs at the beginning of a word even if they were pronounced last. This practice is known as honorific transposition and caused the names of deities to be written first and according to an order of precedence in which Re always took premier place. It is not always possible to sort out this type of muddle and sometimes different versions of the same name may occur which could be equally valid. Once again, classical sources may offer some help in this matter. The common Middle-Kingdom name written as Usert-sen, in which Usert or Wosret is the name of a goddess, was transcribed by the Greeks as Sesostris. This indicates that the Usert element was pronounced last so the name is Senusert, literally 'a man of [dedicated to] Usert'. The name Tutankhamen is written in the order Amen-tut-ankh but its meaning, 'Living Image of Amen', shows that the god's name should be pronounced at the end.

It is not only Greek and Latin that provide pronunciation guides. Foreign rulers corresponded with Egyptian kings using Akkadian, the diplomatic language of the ancient world, which was written in the cuneiform script. Most kings were addressed by their official coronation names which, in their hieroglyphic forms, very often contain the names of two or more deities. It may be difficult to decide which god's name appears where in the order of pronunciation but in Akkadian, as in Greek, the name was written as it sounded to foreign ears. So Amenhotep III was called Nimuria by the King of Babylon in letters preserved in the Amarna archive. The king's coronation name was written in the order Re-Maet-neb but the Akkadian version gives a clear indication that it was pronounced Neb-Maet-Re.

Coptic, being the last spoken version of ancient Egyptian, can also give some guide as to how words may be pronounced. By comparing Coptic words with the alphabetic hieroglyphs it is possible to explain the choice of a sign to represent a particular sound. The Coptic word for 'mouth' is 'ro' and the mouth sign in Egyptian was used for the consonant 'r'. This is a simple principle – 'r' for 'ro' like 'r' for 'rabbit' in English, or 'r' for 'roi' in French. Unfortunately Coptic itself was a dying language, even in Champollion's time, when it was understood and used only by diminishing communities of Coptic Christian monks. It also has to be appreciated that Coptic was the latest and therefore the most corrupt form of the ancient tongue. The language spoken by a Copt and that by a man from the Old Kingdom was separated by more than two thousand years. Compare how much English has changed in the same length of time, not many ordinary people would be able to understand Anglo-Saxon, Old English, or Chaucerian Middle English and even Elizabethan English, as used by Shakespeare, causes many headaches for modern schoolchildren.

Such are some of the complexities of the pronunciation of Egyptian names. It has to be accepted that no one today can accurately vocalize the ancient Egyptian language. Ancient Egyptian cannot be spoken. Such as it remains, it is only a written language that may be read with greater or lesser ease, depending on the style of the script and the period in which it was written. The elements of the language which changed least throughout the 3500 years of dynastic history were names, titles and numbers which makes a study of these an ideal starting point for anyone wishing to learn about the script. Our modern attempts to pronounce ancient Egyptian names are entirely in tune with the Egyptian belief in the power of the name. Twentieth-century accents may be very poor but our intentions are good.

Names, as in modern societies, varied in popularity according to fashion. Some names only occur in certain periods and therefore indicate a particular dynasty or even reign. Some of the commonest names were short, of one or two syllables, and appear to have had no meaning at all, being chosen for their sound. Such names were particularly common in the Old Kingdom when names such as Idi, Pepi and Ipy abound. The name Tiy could be spelled in several ways and is variously transcribed as Ti, Tiyi, Tiye, Tey, Tia, Tuia, Tjuia, Thuya and others. None of these seems to have had any specific meaning and the name in its different forms was used for both boys and girls and in all levels of society. An important court official during the Fifth Dynasty under Kings Neferikare and Niuserre was called Ti. His tomb, which contains many marvellous, detailed reliefs, is in the older part of the Saqqara necropolis. The wife of Amenhotep III was called Tiye and her mother was Tjuia. The wife of Pharaoh Ay was called Tey. These are all modern ways of transcribing what is essentially the same name. At the beginning of the Nineteenth Dynasty a daughter of Seti I, a sister of Ramesses II, was given the name Tia and she married a man of the same name. The Tomb of the Two Tias is in the Memphite necropolis in the same area as that of Horemheb.

The name used by the royal family of the day was always popular: in the later Old Kingdom the names Pepi and Teti were common; in the Middle Kingdom Antef, Amenemhet and Senusert came into vogue; and at the beginning of the New Kingdom the proliferation of Ahmoses, Amenhoteps and Thutmoses is quite bewildering. It will be seen that many of these names include the name of a deity and most have very definite meanings: Amenemhet means 'Amen to the fore'; Ahmose means 'a child born of the moon'; and Amenhotep means 'Amen is satisfied'. For the hieroglyphic forms of the names of the gods see Tables 9 and 10, pages 86 and 87.

To avoid confusion it was common to use an extra epithet, often expressing a relationship, to identify individuals bearing the same given name. At the beginning of the Eighteenth Dynasty, a time when there were more Ahmoses about, both male and female, than one could throw a stick at, a venerable army officer of that name had his biography inscribed in his tomb. There he stated that his father was called Baba, an unusual enough name in itself to be, possibly, a nickname, but he called himself Ahmose, son of Abana, as was the custom, giving his mother's name. The terms which could be used for this type of designation were 'born of' when using the mother's name and 'made by' or 'of his body', when using the father's name. Later in the same dynasty, under Amenhotep III, the architect and government official who was responsible for much of the king's building works in the Theban area, bore the same name as his master. He styled himself 'Amenhotep, son of Hapu'. An archivist of the cult of Anubis in the reign of Thutmose IV had the same name as the king but was known as Pa-ry after his maternal uncle who was also his father-in-law.

Amenhotep, Amenemhet and any other names including the element Amen were very commonly abbreviated to Ameny. Mery, meaning 'beloved', was the usual diminutive of such names as Meryatum, Meryre and Meryptah. Some names were simply the names of deities without any epithets or adjectives attached. Iset (Isis) and Hathor were popular girls' names. This was not thought to be blasphemous at all, any more than the Spanish use of Jesus as a personal name, or the use of Muhammad in its various forms in the Islamic world, might be considered irreverent nowadays. No thought is given to the shortening of Christ in Christopher or Christine to Chris, so the diminutive form of Hathor which, for some obscure reason was Hunero, should not be surprising.

Nicknames were not always abbreviations or diminutives. In some cases it is possible to attribute an additional name to something as simple as the place of birth, so Ahmose Pa-Nekheb means Ahmose from Nekheb, but other names for common use are not so obviously explained. For instance, the name Amenhotep was sometimes replaced by Huy or Huya as in the case of the Viceroy of Nubia who took up his office in the reign of Tutankhamen. Perhaps this represents an Egyptian equivalent to the English practice of calling many people named Miller, 'Dusty', and all Wilsons, 'Tug' –

and the reasons for the Egyptian equivalents were probably just as lost to the ancients as some of the modern versions are to us.

Other nicknames may well have been family endearments. Simut, an accountant of cattle at the Amen temple of Karnak, was known as Kyky. His name is written as 'Simut say of him Kyky', which is best translated as Simut, known as Kyky (fig.12). It is not hard to imagine a young brother or sister, unable to say the new baby's proper name, calling him Kyky, and the name sticking.

12. The titles and names of Amenemhet whose nickname was Surer, from his tomb in Thebes.

Translation: The Hereditary Prince and Nomarch, greatest of the Favoured, Acquaintance of the Lord of the Two Lands, King's Scribe, he who is at the head of the King, Amen-em-het, say of him, Surer, justified.

Names like this, being used constantly in place of given names, seem to have been common in ancient Egypt. A young man shown in the tomb of Paheri at el-Kab, was called Pa-miw, 'the Cat'. It is hard to imagine why he should have been given such a name at birth but it could have been adopted as a reference to his fastidious nature, or his stealthy tread, or any other cat-like trait. The wife of the gardener Nakht at Thebes was called Ta-hemet which can mean 'the servant' or even 'the slave'. This is a very unlikely, even unkind name with which to label a child, but then in Egyptian the same word stem is used to mean Majesty in the epithet 'His Majesty', so *hemet*, with its feminine ending, could mean something like Queenie which is far more acceptable.

Mose, meaning 'born of', was a frequently used element in personal names, like Minmose (born of Min), Amenmose (born of Amen) and Merymose (beloved birth). Ramesses, the name now used for the kings of the Nineteenth and Twentieth Dynasties, is only a royal variant of the common name Ramose (born of Re). Sometimes there is no difference in the way the name is written for a king or a commoner but modern convention is to call a king Ramesses and a commoner Ramose. By itself, Mose was often used as a boy's name in the peasant population and was a recognized abbreviation for any name in which it occurred. This is still evident in the Middle East where the Egyptian Mose became the Biblical

13. A wife makes a funerary offering of linen to her husband. From the tomb of Sennefer, Mayor of Thebes in the reign of Amenhotep II.

Translation (right to left): His sister [wife] Meryt, making a presentation of linen to the Mayor of the Southern City [Thebes], Sen-nefer, justified

Moses, then the Hebrew Moshe and the Arabic Musa. This is a rare example of the survival of an ancient Egyptian word into modern usage.

The commonest names were the simplest, often being no more than adjectives like User (strong), Nedjem (sweet) and Nefer (good or beautiful). When used as a girl's name, an adjective should take the feminine 't' ending but this is not always written.

In the list of adjectives in the first table dealing with elements found in personal names, each word is given in its masculine form. The heading for Tables 1–3 reads 'their names are caused to live'.

Any adjective could be linked with other words or the name of a deity to create a phrase such as Mutnefert ('Mut is Beautiful', or 'Beautiful as Mut') or Amen-user ('Amen is Strong') (fig.13).

Some names ran in families and it was common for children to be named after their parents. From lists in some tombs it would appear that several children of the same parents were given the same name. This may well be a symptom of the high infant-

mortality rate and possibly only one child of any given name survived into adulthood. In the Sixth Dynasty the Vizier Djau had at least five brothers who all seem to have had the same name. Their two sisters were both called Ankh-es-en-Meryre, which means 'Her life belongs to Meryre', but this was as a result of a deliberate change of name for both ladies were married to King Pepi I whose throne name was Meryre. This helps make sense of the adopted name.

The Egyptians liked to keep honoured names in the family. On a Middle-Kingdom cenotaph from Saqqara which is now in the Cairo Museum, three brothers all named Sekwaskhet are differentiated by means of second names or epithets; they are called Aa (great or senior), Hery-ib (he who is in the middle) and Nedjes (small). This eminently practical if unimaginative means of naming children is no different from the Roman practice of using ordinal numbers (Primus, Secundus, Tertius) as names. The grandson of Sekwaskhet-Aa was also called Sekwaskhet.

The tradition of giving children within the same family the same second name is still quite common. The children of noble European families often use both parents' family names to indicate dynastic links. Spanish children have always acquired a string of family names and in nineteenth-century England, Queen Victoria gave all her sons the name Albert and every daughter had Victoria among their many first names.

14. The daughter of King Teti who became the wife of the Vizier Mereruka. As well as having a formal, royal name she was known by a 'beautiful name' or nickname.

Translation: King's daughter, of his body, Priestess of Hathor, Lady of the Sycamore, Har-watet-khet, her beautiful name is Sesh-seshet

In other cases of duplication, the family might have used nicknames to identify children who had the same birth name. Such an identifying name was called a 'good' or 'beautiful name' – 'ren nefer'. If a child bore the same name as a parent it may well have been differentiated by the epithet 'pa-sheri', (masc) or 'ta-sherit' (fem), meaning 'younger' or 'junior'. On the false-door stela of Kaihap in the British Museum, it is possible to identify his eldest son,

	mery	beloved		wer	great
	mer, mi	beloved		aa	great
	nefer	good, beautiful		netjer	divine
	nakht	strong		user	powerful, strong
	hotep	satisfied, pleased		mes, mose	born
	setep	chosen		hesy	favoured
	tepy	first, chief		imakh	revered, venerated
	khenty	foremost		keni	brave, strong
	nedjem	sweet		renpi	young, flourishing
	wab	pure		seneb	healthy
	sheps	noble		djeser	sacred, holy
	nub	gold		hedj	white, silver, bright

Table 1: Elements in Personal Names (adjectives)

Kaihap Junior and his favourite grandson, Kaihap III. One of the six Amarna princesses was named Neferneferuaten ta-sherit. Her mother, Nefertiti, was given the name Neferneferuaten on the occasion of one of her husband's jubilees so the little princess could not have been named 'junior' until after this event. This is the sort of evidence which may be used to date inscriptions within a reign.

Although there is very little evidence that the Egyptians celebrated birthdays, some names are indicative of a child being born at a certain time of year. The ending '-em-heb' means 'in festival', so Hor-em-heb means 'Horus is in festival', implying that the birth occurred at the time of one of the feast days of the god Horus. When the cult statue of a god was paraded as part of a religious celebration, it was carried in a miniature sacred bark known as a *wiya*, so suffixing a god's name '-em-wiya' (in his/her sacred bark) was another way of denoting a festival day. Thus Mut-em-wiya indicates the time of a festival of the goddess Mut. Of course, if such a name is used by several generations it is unlikely that every person of that name was born at the same time of year. By modern analogy, although some children born at Christmas time are called Noël or Holly, not all those so-named have birthdays in December; neither are all Pascals likely to have been born at Easter. Having been given a name which included the name of a deity, an Egyptian might well have paid particular reverence to that god, and just as the French recognize their personal saints' days or fetes, the Egyptians might have had certain days of the calendar which they celebrated as personal holidays.

Names could be changed or added on special occasions or as a mark of distinction. In the Old Kingdom it was not unusual for a king to grant his most-valued court officials permission to include his name in their own. This caused some private individuals to have part of their names enclosed in a cartouche, though this does not necessarily imply that they were in any way related to the royal family. The Jubilee or Heb Sed was a great occasion for changing names. A district governor in the reign of Pepi II was known as Pepi-en-Heb-Sed ('Pepi is in Jubilee') and the overseer of the royal necropolis in the same period was Degem known as Pepi-mer ('Beloved of Pepi') (fig.15).

15. A Fifth Dynasty courtier who was granted the honour of including the king's name in his own. From a relief in the Luxor Museum.

Translation: King's Acquaintance, Chamberlain of the South, Overseer of the Double Granary, (Wenis)-ankh

With other names occurring so frequently it was also common practice for a courtier to be given a distinguishing 'good name' like the majordomo of the royal palace under Pepi II, whose names appear at the head of this chapter. He was 'Idi whose good name is Tep-em-kau' ('Best of Souls'). However it is not so obvious why the King's Scribe and Treasurer, Djehuti-mose, in the reign of Amenhotep II, should have been known as Djehuti-nefer. The change in name is so slight as to be hardly important.

Some names tell a story. The girl called Ankh-mut-es, meaning 'her mother lives', could have been so-named because she was the 'spitting image of her mother', or it is quite possible that her mother died giving birth so that the baby girl was seen to replace her mother in the family's affections. In the Fourth Dynasty a baby born a dwarf was named Seneb meaning 'healthy', which may have been a wish for his survival by his doting mother. If so, it was a wish that came true. In spite of his physical problems Seneb became chief of the royal linen works, was married to a woman who had the title Princess (equivalent to the Honourable or perhaps Lady), and had at least two normal-sized children. His delightful family statue is now in the Cairo Museum.

In the Turin Papyrus which contains the transcripts of the trials of the conspirators in a plot to assassinate Ramesses III, some names were deliberately changed. No one would have called a child Mesedsure ('Re Hates Him'). It is far more likely that the man bore the common name Meryre ('Beloved of Re') but that this was considered a blasphemy for someone who had been involved in an attempt to murder the living god. Another conspirator was mentioned by the name of Bin-em-Wase ('Evil in Thebes'). It is probable that his real name was Kha-em-Wase ('Glory in Thebes') which was a popular personal name of that period. A third criminal was not even given an alternative name which probably indicates he was of a lower class than the others. He was called simply Pa-nek, 'the serpent' or 'the evil-doer' which must have been another derogatory pseudonym. A son of Ramesses III was also on trial. He was given the name Pentaware which meant something like 'the fugitive'. Deprived of the decent royal name he had undoubtedly had since birth, he was even more reviled than the others in the conspiracy, for his crime, plotting against his own father, was greater than theirs.

At the beginning of the Nineteenth Dynasty the ruling family inherited the family name Seti, 'one of the god Seth'. Seth (Set or Sutekh) was a god with a rather ambiguous identity. (fig. 16). He was traditionally one of the two patron gods of Egypt in partnership with Horus, but he was also the murderer of Osiris and so the implacable enemy of Osiris's son Horus. In the temple built by Seti I to the god Osiris, and in his tomb where he hoped to be joined with Osiris in the next life, he could hardly portray the god's murderer over and over again as he would have done had he written his name in its Sethian form. Instead, in the cartouche of his personal name, the Seth beast was replaced by the figure of Osiris himself. Words had power and names were the most powerful of all words.

16. Relief from the tomb of Seti I in the Valley of Kings. The king's name is here written with the symbol of the god Osiris replacing that of the god Seth. Hovering above the king's head is the vulture goddess Nekhebt.

Translation: Goddess, Nekhebt, the White One of Nekhen, given health, life and dominion

Columns from right to left

1. The Living Good God, Son of Amen, born of Mut, Lady of. . . .
2. Asheru [the lake in the southern part of the Karnak precinct] in the palace of Ipet Esut
3. The Osiris King, Lord of the Two Lands (Men-Maet-Re)
4. Son of Re, of his body, his beloved, Lord of Appearances (Seti Mer-en-Ptah)
5. True of Voice [justified] before Osiris, Foremost of the West.

Tables 2 and 3 which follow give further elements of personal names and some other useful expressions such as terms of relationship. These, together with the alphabetic signs, the adjectives and the names of deities which will be found in Tables 9 and 10, pages 86 and 87, should enable the reader to transcribe most of the commonly occurring names and designations to be found on personal monuments.

	it	father		mut	mother
	sheri(t)	younger, junior		chred	child
	sa(t)	son, daughter		sen(et)	brother sister
	neb(et)	lord, master lady		henut	mistress
	bak(et)	manservant maidservant		tut	image
	neferu	beauty		ankh	life
	maet	truth, order justice		khopsh	arm, strength
	maet	truth, order justice		pehti	strength
	kha	glory, appearance		waskhet	great hall (of temple)
	heb	festival		wiya	sacred bark (of a god)
	kheper	form, shape		ib	heart, wish desire
	hat	front		pet	sky, heaven

Table 2: Elements in Personal Names (nouns)

	pa	the, this (masc.)		ta	the, this (fem.)
	sw	he, him		set	she, her
	-ef	he, his (suffix)		-es	she, her (suffix)
	-u (m) -ut (f)	plural ending		em	in, from, of, at
	en	belongs to, of		imy	being in, within
	enty	who, which		er	to, at
	em-khet	accompanying, after		hir	upon, on
	mi	like		kher	near, with above, over
	kheft	in front of, before		khent	in front of, over
	hery	over, above		kha	behind, around
	mes-en	born of (followed by mother's name)		ir-en	born to (followed by father's name)
	neb	each, every, all		en-khet	of the body

Table 3: Elements in Personal Names (pronouns, prepositions etc.)

3. ROYALTY

In the context of ancient Egypt the term 'document' refers more often to a text carved in stone than to one written on papyrus. The hieroglyphic documents which survive from the earliest periods are very different from the monumental inscriptions which are regarded as characteristic of the Egyptian civilization. The oldest documents are frequently fragmentary, usually very short and are composed of a limited number of hieroglyphs. Although many of these signs continued in use for thousands of years, it is not always possible to interpret their use in primitive, early texts. One reason for this is that writing, in its infancy, was rarely used to convey continuous or narrative language.

The knowledge of reading and writing was possessed only by an élite who used these skills to demonstrate their power and authority. The documents they produced were principally statements of that power, being used above all to indicate ownership. Inscriptions were carved on the lintels, door jambs and stelae of monuments, and on ivory and wooden labels which were attached to the baskets and boxes used to store possessions. The most important element of any such inscription was the name of the owner of the building or item so marked. The most powerful owner of all was the king. Other signs might have changed in form and purpose over the centuries but the way in which the king's name was written became enshrined in Egyptian tradition so that royal names may still be identified as such, even within otherwise unreadable inscriptions.

It is hardly surprising that the most powerful individual of the state should have more names than any other. Two of the five Great Names of the classic royal titulary were in use at the very beginning of the First Dynasty. Two more names have their origins in that same period, although their style was not formalized until later, and the fifth name was brought into common use in the Fourth Dynasty. The first 'date' in Egyptian history, at least as far as Egyptologists are concerned, is that of the Unification of the Two Lands which is currently thought to have been accomplished around 3100 BC. This conventionally marks the bringing together under one monarch of two separate states now known as Upper and Lower Egypt, (the Southern Nile Valley and the Northern Delta respectively).

Traditionally the king who effected this political union was the ruler of Upper Egypt, named by Herodotus as Menes, who conquered his northern neighbours in battle and thus became the first 'Lord of the Two Lands'. A huge commemorative palette made of green schist records just such a conquest by a king with the name Narmer. This palette, now in the Cairo Museum, had been buried in the Horus Temple at Hierakonpolis, along with many other commemorative items which may have been presented to the god as offerings indicating the power and prestige of their donors. These objects are also documents in Egyptological terms even though the hieroglyphs they bear are sparse and antiquated. None of the objects found in what has come to be known as the 'Main Deposit' bears much more than a few hieroglyphs. These are scattered throughout a pictorial representation of events in a way similar to that of the elementary text running through the Bayeux Tapestry, only less informative. The picture or relief tells the real story. The written words are most often used to identify people by name or title, rather like labelling the important features of a diagram, and the most important person portrayed is always the king.

The King of the Unification seems to have originated in the south and was a worshipper of the hawk-god Horus. He, not unnaturally, put himself under the protection of his patron deity and was known as The Horus, an earthly incarnation of the great sky-god who later became confused or amalgamated with Horus the son of Osiris. The Horus falcon perched on a religious standard was used as the hieroglyph for the royal, third-person singular pronoun, 'he' or 'his', when referring to the king. The Horus name is the earliest

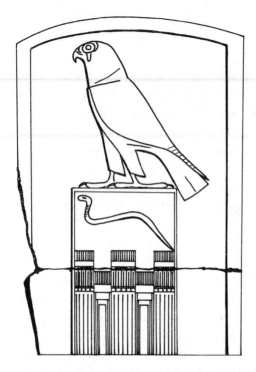

royal name to be used and it was written not in a cartouche but in a distinctive rectangular enclosure called a *serekh* (fig. 17). This enclosure represents the royal residence being viewed from the front and from above at the same time. The lower part of the rectangle is decorated to represent the panelled façade of the king's palace while the upper open space is the plan of the inner courtyard. Perched on the roof of the palace is the Horus falcon who thus protects the building and its occupant, the king, who is represented by his name in hieroglyphs written within the courtyard. In one example only, shown at the head of this chapter, the talons of the hawk extend through the roof of the *serekh* to grasp the hieroglyphs of a shield and a mace which make up the sign for 'to fight'. This is how the name of the King Aha, successor to Narmer, was written. Perhaps his name should better be transcribed as Hor-aha, 'The Fighting Hawk', since clearly the falcon symbol plays a more integral part in this name than in other Horus names. Tombs of both Narmer and Hor-aha have been identified and various labels and jar sealings bear their names, but it is still uncertain which, if either, of them may be identified with the legendary Menes.

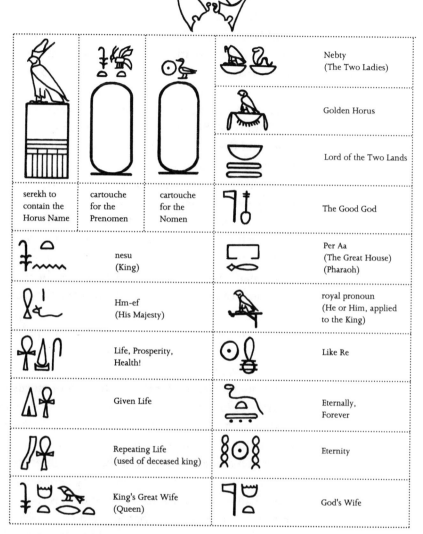

				Nebty (The Two Ladies)
				Golden Horus
				Lord of the Two Lands
serekh to contain the Horus Name	cartouche for the Prenomen	cartouche for the Nomen		The Good God
	nesu (King)			Per Aa (The Great House) (Pharaoh)
	Hm-ef (His Majesty)			royal pronoun (He or Him, applied to the King)
	Life, Prosperity, Health!			Like Re
	Given Life			Eternally, Forever
	Repeating Life (used of deceased king)			Eternity
	King's Great Wife (Queen)			God's Wife

Table 4: Royal Names and Titles

Recent research has cast doubt upon the existence of a state of Lower Egypt as such before the Unification. It is now suggested that the origins of the kingdom were in the southern Nagada culture and monuments ascribed to the first kings of the dual state have been found at the southern power-centres of Hierakonpolis, Ombos and Abydos. The twinning of deities, crowns and heraldic symbols associated with royalty seems to have been a reflection of the Egyptian concept of balance or *maet* which is often translated as 'truth' or 'justice'. The country itself was differentiated as desert or cultivated land, neither of which could exist without the other. The falcon Horus was countered by an alter ego Seth, their attributes of order and chaos being considered necessary to a balanced state. In coronation or jubilee scenes, Horus and Seth are shown as supporters of the king, conferring upon him the two crowns, the 'Red' and the 'White', which are shown at the head of Table 4 which gives royal names and titles.

The 'Red Crown', associated with Horus, is conventionally called the 'Crown of Lower Egypt', whereas this god's principal cult centres are in the south, and Narmer, a follower of Horus, is shown wearing the 'White Crown'. The persistence of the concept of the 'Two Lands' centuries after the 'Unification' makes no sense unless it is a manifestation of a dualistic view of the world rather than a statement of political demarcation. Thus the wearer of the 'Double Crown', who is usually described as 'King of Upper and Lower Egypt', was simply the ruler of a realm in equilibrium and he could not have been crowned with the 'Red' without also being crowned with the 'White'.

Putting himself under the protection of Horus the king also commended himself to Seth. This aspect of duality was demonstrated in the Second Dynasty when King Peribsen chose to have the mythical Seth beast depicted in place of the Horus falcon on the serekh of his official name. This has been interpreted as an indication of a religious revolution but in reality Peribsen chose to use the other half of an inseparable pair of deities to introduce his name. In fact, it is highly likely that he used two serekh names, the other being the classic Horus name, Sekhemib. This use of two names would make perfect sense as does the name adopted by the last king of the dynasty, Kha-sekhemwy, whose serekh was surmounted by both the falcon and the Seth animal. The name Kha-sekhemwy is itself suggestive of this equilibrium. It means 'the Appearance of the Two Powers' (fig. 18).

The character of the first kings of the dual state as described by Herodotus and Manetho is probably a composite constructed from folk memories of the reigns of at least two of these early kings. None of the Horus names of the First Dynasty bears any resemb-

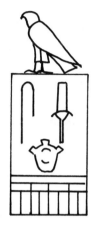

18. Three *serekhs* illustrating the changes in the style of this name during the Second Dynasty. Those to left and centre appear to have belonged to the same king.

Translation (reading left to right):
1. Seth Name: Per-ib-sen
2. Horus Name: Sekhem-ib
3. Horus-Seth Name: Kha-sekhemwy

lance to the Hellenized name Menes, but a clue to his identity may be found in the second of the Great Names, the name introduced by the symbols of a vulture and a cobra, each perched on a basket. These represented the vulture-goddess Nekhebt, wearer of the 'White Crown', and the cobra-goddess Wadjet, wearer of the 'Red Crown'. The basket hieroglyph means 'Lord' or 'Lady' and together the goddesses are known as the 'Two Ladies' or Nebty. The Nebty name was not written in any special enclosure but is identified accompanying the Horus name of both Narmer and Hor-aha, as in the chapter heading. In each of these earliest cases the hieroglyph used for the name itself was a gaming board set up ready for play. This meant 'established' and was pronounced 'men'. It does not take a giant leap of imagination to understand how this could have been read by the Greeks as Menes. The use of the two goddesses is further emphasis of the twofold nature of the kingship. Nekhebt and Wadjet are called the patron goddesses of Upper and Lower Egypt. Although Nekhebt's principal shrine was in the south and Wadjet's in the north it is not necessary to set geographical limits on their authority. The king claimed the protection of both goddesses in the same way that he claimed the protection of Horus and Seth since the Nebty could be considered as female counterparts of the two gods. From the brow of the funerary mask of Tutankhamen the heads of the vulture and the cobra face the king's potential enemies defying any attack on their protégé. In many royal reliefs the vulture is shown hovering above the king, her wings outspread in an attitude of protection, while repeated figures of the cobra form a frieze above the whole scene (see fig.16, page 45).

The third name is of less obvious origin. It is introduced by the figure of a falcon perched on the symbol for gold and so is called the Golden Horus name. It is thought that gold, being imperishable, unchanging and valuable, was emblematic of the nature of the monarchy. Combined with the falcon, a synonym for king, the gold stresses the value and permanence of the kingship. In the very earliest period the symbols may have been used as one of the many important epithets of the king rather than to introduce a name. One of the earliest examples of the Golden Horus name is found on a fragment of a stone vase now in the Metropolitan Museum of Art in New York. It shows the falcon and gold symbols and is associated with the Nebty name of Qaa, the last king of the First Dynasty. Very often, in later periods, the Nebty and Golden Horus names and even, on occasion, the Horus name are only slight variations on the same theme (fig.19).

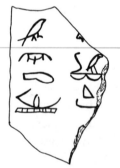

19. Fragment of a stone jar bearing the _Nebty_ and Golden Horus names of King Ka of the First Dynasty.

The fourth name in the king's titulary ultimately became the most important, supplanting the Horus name in its use for official purposes. It also emphasized the duality of the kingdom by its heading which comprised two heraldic emblems, the sedge reed and the bee. The title is now translated as King of Upper and Lower Egypt. In Egyptian terms it meant 'He of the Sedge and the Bee', Nesu-bit. This too, in its earliest manifestation, may have been used as a title rather than as an introduction to a name. This is indicated by the fact that either of the two symbols could be used for the word 'king'. Nesu, 'He of the Reed', was the commonest word used for the noun 'king' as opposed to a title. Bity, 'He of the Bee', was employed in official titles such as 'King's Seal-Bearer'. It is pointless to contemplate why these particular emblems should have been chosen to represent the two parts of Egypt, the sedge for the south and the bee for the north. They had been used for that purpose for so long that even the Egyptians themselves probably could not have explained their origins. It was simply enough to know what they represented when using them as writing signs (fig.20).

20. A Third-Dynasty sculptor's trial piece, from Hurbeit in the eastern Delta. The relief shows the two introductory titles for the *Nesu-bit* (above) and *Nebty* (below) names. Metropolitan Museum of Arts, New York.

As with other references to the dual state, it was impossible to be Nesu without also being Bity. The use of one by itself was not necessarily indicative of the kingship of only half of the country, nor did it refer to the area of origin of the royal house. The full title was used to introduce the most commonly used of all royal names which was enclosed in a cartouche. This was the name taken by the king at his accession and conferred upon him at his coronation. This practice was similar to the choice of an official name by a new Pope or the decision in 1936 of the British prince, known as Bertie to his family, to become King as George VI. The Nesu-bit name was used in all official texts from inscriptions to everyday accounts. It was the name used by foreign rulers when corresponding with the King of Egypt. The name chosen was a religious statement, most often relating the king to some aspect or attribute of the sun-god Re.

There are very few examples of a duplicated coronation name, which is also referred to as the *prenomen*. Sometimes a king would deliberately imitate a worthy predecessor by adopting a *prenomen* similar in form to that of his chosen model. This is very apparent in the coronation name of the first king of the Nineteenth Dynasty which echoes that of the founding ruler of the Eighteenth Dynasty: compare Men-pehti-Re (Ramesses I) with Neb-pehti-Re (Ahmose).

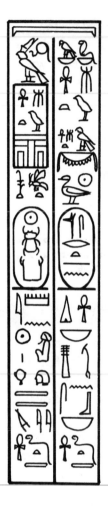

Since it was extremely rare for two kings to have the same official name, the Egyptians had a unique label for each of their monarchs. Learning and remembering these in sequence would be a true feat of memory for modern students of Egyptology. The name by which an Egyptian king is known today is most often the fifth of the Great Names, the name he was given as a child. This is called the *nomen* and was written in a cartouche introduced by the term 'Son of Re'. It was during the Fourth Dynasty that the Son of Re name was first used to imply divine origin, linking the earthly ruler with the supreme solar deity. The name given to a prince could be any of the names used by the population as a whole, though there was a tendency to follow a family tradition of acknowledging one particular deity, perhaps the god of the home town of the ruling house; this was the case with the Eleventh Dynasty whose origins were in Thebes, the home of the war-god Montu, hence the name Montuhotep. The birth name was not enclosed in a cartouche unless and until the prince became king and then he might have had a regal epithet added to stress his new status. The combination of *prenomen* and *nomen* was enough to differentiate one king from another. The use of Roman numerals after the Son of Re names is a modern convention which helps to identify kings of the same given name and to place their reigns in chronological order. The hiero-glyphic version of a Son of Re name does not include a numeral (fig.21).

21. The Five Great Names of Senusert I, from the way-station in the Open Air Museum at Karnak. The two columns of hieroglyphs are surmounted by the hieroglyph for 'sky' or 'heaven'.

Translation (columns read left to right):
1. Horus [Ankh-mesu]; *Nesu-bit* (Kheper-ka-Re), beloved of Amen-Re, Chief over the Two Lands, living forever . . .
2. *Nebty*, Ankh-mesu; Golden Horus, Ankh-mesu; Son of Re, (Sen-Usert), given all Life, Stability and Dominion, and all Health, living forever

Some of the introductory titles to the two cartouche names had alternatives or were given additional epithets which came into fashion in the New Kingdom and were used in various combina-tions by most later kings. The *prenomen* could be introduced by the expression 'Lord of the Two Lands' in place of the sedge and

22. Alexander the Great shown as the King of Egypt in the sanctuary of the Temple of Amen at Karnak. The introductory titles to his names are in the later style adopted during the New Kingdom and his personal name is 'spelled' out phonetically.

Translation: King of Upper and Lower Egypt, Lord of the Two Lands, (Setep-en-Re, Mery-Amen); Son of Re, Lord of Appearances, (A-L-K-S-I-N-D-R-S), beloved of Amen-Re, Lord of the Thrones of the Two Lands.

the bee, and could also be preceded by the title 'the Good God', the king being considered a god on earth. The nomen could have the epithet 'Lord of Appearances' added to or replacing the 'Son of Re' introduction. Sometimes the traditional titles were omitted altogether and each of the two cartouches was placed on the symbol for gold and topped by the sun's disc encircled by two serpents who represented the Nebty. Other epithets commonly followed the cartouches. These might include 'Given Life', 'Appearing like Re in the Sky' and 'Living Forever' (fig.22).

Some epithets were used in the special context of the festival which was celebrated on the thirtieth anniversary of the king's

accession to the throne and thereafter every three or four years. The Jubilee or Heb Sed was a re-enactment of the king's coronation at which he was reconfirmed as ruler of the dual state and received the blessings of all the most important national deities. Just as the coronation had been an occasion for taking new names, the Jubilee was a time for changing or adding to those names, and in the case of a ruler who had celebrated several jubilees it is possible to date a document to a specific part of his reign by identifying in it the particular forms of the names he used or the epithets attached to them. The obelisk of Thutmose III, which is now in Istanbul, was clearly erected as part of one of the King's Jubilee celebrations since his names were followed by the epithet 'Lord of Jubilees'.

The most dramatic change of name took place when Amenhotep IV completely altered his nomen from Amenhotep (Amen is Satisfied) to Akhenaten (Beneficial to Aten). More commonly the Horus, Nebty and Golden Horus names were those which were changed. The king recognized by future generations as the founder of the Middle Kingdom was Montuhotep I. He came to the throne after what is now known as the First Intermediate Period, a time during which the government had disintegrated and Egypt had been ruled by local princes who occasionally claimed the kingship but whose authority had been strictly limited. Members of a powerful family from the Theban area had managed to exert their influence over a widening area until one of them, Montuhotep, had become powerful enough to bring together an army to conquer the residue of fragmented government in the north. When he first took the throne as 'King of the Two Lands' he chose, as his Horus name, Se-ankh-ib-tawy, ('He who Causes the Heart of the Two Lands to Live'). Later, presumably when he felt he really had earned the kingship, he changed his Horus name to Neb-en-Hedj ('Lord of the White Crown'), and finally, when he had been fully accepted as ruler of the dual state, his Horus name was changed again to Sem-tawy ('He who Unites the Two Lands'). This use of three distinct Horus names has been confusing and it was not always realized that they belonged to one and the same king. Sometimes he is named as Montuhotep II and the first of his Horus names is ascribed to another Montuhotep, a supposed predecessor. This means that

some references give four kings of this name belonging to the Eleventh Dynasty whereas more recent works indicate only three. Usually he is designated by his coronation name Neb-hepet-Re Montuhotep to avoid confusion.

The obelisk in the square of St John Lateran in Rome bears the complete titulary of Thutmose III on its four faces, but the names appear in two different versions (fig.23). The obelisk was apparently commissioned late in the king's fifty-four-year reign. The king's titles include a reference to his domination of Egypt's traditional enemies, the Nine Bows. Thutmose III was a warrior king and his conquests expanded the Egyptian empire to its greatest extent. It is not to be wondered that he should acknowledge this success in his choice of names. It is not so obvious why he should have changed his Horus name from 'Mighty Bull Arising in Thebes', to 'Mighty Bull, Beloved of Re'. The term 'mighty' or 'victorious bull' was a popular royal epithet from earliest times when on the Narmer palette the king is portrayed as a bull trampling his enemies.

23. Two versions of the names of Thutmose III as shown on the obelisk which is now in the square of St John Lateran in Rome.

Translation: Far left: Horus, [strong bull appearing in Thebes]; *Nebty*, Enduring like Re in the sky; Golden Horus, Holy of appearances, powerful, strong; *Nesu-bit*, (Men-kheper-Re, Setep-en-Re); Son of Re, (Thutmose Nefer-kheper)
Left: Horus, [Strong bull, beloved of Re]; *Nebty*, Great of worth in all lands; Golden Horus, Strong of arm over the Nine Bows; *Nesu-bit*, (Men-kheper-Re); Son of Re, (Thutmose Nefer-kheper)

A title which emerged during the later dynasties is that of Per-aa which was used as a euphemism for 'king'. Originally it meant the Great House, referring to the royal residence. Gradually its meaning changed to encompass the idea of a central government building, the seat of political as well as royal power, just as we understand the use of terms like the 'White House' or 'Number Ten'. Eventually it was applied to the king himself providing the scribes with a useful and respectful term in place of cumbersome titles or the repetitive use of 'His Majesty'. Thus decrees were issued by the Per-aa. Of course, it was never believed that the Great House spoke any more than a Buckingham Palace statement is thought to be the words of a building. The Greeks found the designation Per-aa a much neater title than the more traditional versions and they used it always in its Hellenized form, Pharaoh.

In the king's tomb or funerary and mortuary monuments, he would be referred to as deceased by the use of the prefix the 'Osiris King', meaning 'the dead king', and the epithets 'True of Voice' (Justified), or 'Repeating Life'. In many cases the king's consort would have shared her husband's tomb but certain royal ladies were granted tombs of their own. In the First Dynasty Neith-hotep the wife of Narmer was buried in a tomb at Nagada which was bigger and more magnificent than that which has been identified as belonging to her husband. It is thought that she outlived him and her burial was prepared by Hor-aha who was, in all probability, her son. It is his name rather than that of Narmer which appears most often on items from Neith-hotep's burial. Another royal lady of the First Dynasty, Mery-neith, has been identified as the owner of two regal tombs, one at Nagada and the other at Saqqara. The way in which her name is written, in a form of *serekh* surmounted by the crossed arrows of the goddess Neith, and the similarity in size and style of her tombs to those of kings of the same period lead to the conclusion that Mery-Neith was more than a king's consort. She was quite probably the first Queen Regnant of ancient Egypt.

The last king of the Second Dynasty, Kha-sekhemwy, was married to a lady who was to be revered in later years as the ancestor of the Third Dynasty. Her name was Ne-Maet-hap and the title she bore was Mut-mes-nesu which could be translated as 'Mother of the King's Children' or 'King-Bearing Mother'. If the latter translation is to be understood, the title could not have been conferred upon Ne-Maet-hap until one of her sons had become king. The adoption after the event of a title claiming official status for a king's mother is not unique. In the Eighteenth Dynasty Queen Mutemwiya, mother of Amenhotep III, was not called 'King's Chief Wife' until after her son had become king himself. This claim was more for Amenhotep's benefit than hers!

In the Old Kingdom, kings of the Fourth to Sixth Dynasties built subsidiary pyramids for their wives close to their own tombs.

Though these pyramids are considerably smaller than those built for the kings themselves, none the less they mark the importance of the women buried beneath them. The wife of Menkaure of the Fourth Dynasty was buried in one of the three lesser pyramids beside that of her husband at Giza. She is portrayed in several beautiful statues which were installed in the king's Valley Temple where she is shown as the king's wife or in the guise of Hathor, the goddess of love. Her name was Khamerynebty and she was the daughter of Khaefre, the builder of the second pyramid at Giza. Menkaure's daughter, though not a child of Khamerynebty, was Khentkhaus, who was married to Userkaf, the first king of the Fifth Dynasty. She bore the title 'Mother of the Two Kings of Upper and Lower Egypt' which refers to her sons Sahure and Neferikare. This title cannot have been conferred upon her until both her children had taken the throne. Her tomb, in the form of a large sarcophagus-shaped structure, was also built at Giza and her mortuary-cult was continued long after the deaths of her sons. She was the physical link between the Fourth and Fifth Dynasties and was revered as a matriarchal figure.

The wives of the Sixth-Dynasty kings were accorded small pyramids within the burial complexes of their husbands. Their names are known but none of them seems to have held any position of power apart from Ankh-es-en-Meryre, wife of Pepi I and mother of Pepi II, who acted as her son's regent in his minority. At the end of the reign of Pepi II – he lived to be nearly one hundred years old – the government of the country collapsed. One of the ephemeral rulers who emerged from the chaos was a woman whom Manetho called Nitocris. He described her as 'the noblest and loveliest woman of her time'. Nitocris held full royal titles. Her *Nesu-bit* name was Net-ikerty ('She who is Excellent'), and her second cartouche, introduced by the simple term 'king', was Menkare, echoing the title of the Fourth-Dynasty king in whose pyramid she was said to have been buried.

Daughters and wives of Middle-Kingdom kings were also provided with lesser pyramids in which they were buried with full royal honours, including the provision of magnificent jewellery. Several collections of jewellery have been recovered from Twelfth-

Dynasty pyramids at Lisht and Hawara on the edge of the Fayum. Many pieces include in their design the names of their owners or the ruling monarch and some were perhaps never worn in life, but were provided as amuletic protection in the next world.

The royal consorts at the beginning of the New Kingdom often took the title 'God's Wife'. There is some evidence that this was a religious title though in most cases it meant the 'Chief Wife of the King'. There was no term in the Egyptian language equivalent to Queen. The consort of the king was known simply as the 'Great Wife of the King'. She might also have been 'King's Daughter' or 'King's Sister'. There were other women who bore the title 'King's Wife' or 'King's Favourite' but the 'Great Royal Wife' took precedence over them all. In royal portraits she was shown with her husband, often on a smaller scale, but always in a prominent position either standing or seated at his side, sometimes with her arm about his waist. She wore the vulture cap of the goddess Mut, consort of the Theban god Amen, and upon that a diadem formed of uraeus serpents. The full crown of the Chief Wife consisted of the horns of Isis or Hathor between which were two plumes and the sun's disc. Her name was written in a cartouche and her titles included 'Lady of the Two Lands', and 'Lady Greatly Beloved of Favour, Grace and Sweetness'. If a royal consort survived her husband to see her son become king, she became Queen Dowager under the title 'King's Mother'.

The most beautifully decorated tomb provided for a royal lady is that of Nefertari, 'Chief Wife' of Ramesses II. It was one of the first tombs to be excavated in what is now called the Valley of Queens where royal wives and children were buried from the Nineteenth Dynasty onwards. In Nefertari's tomb, the absence of the figure of her husband is notable, especially considering his predilection for displaying his own name prominently on every monument he built. It is the Queen who is shown offering to the gods and being led by Isis and Hathor before Osiris. Her name is everywhere boldly inscribed, Nefertari-Mery-en-Mut (fig.24).

There were no single titles equivalent to Prince or Princess. Royal children were designated as sons or daughters of the king. In most cases, the names of their mothers are not mentioned and often

24. Queen Nefertari, wife of Ramesses II, as shown in her tomb in the 'Valley of Queens'. She wears the vulture cap of the goddess Mut surmounted by the coronet with twin plumes, the crown of the Queen Consort of Egypt.

Translation: For recitation by Osiris, '[She is] the Great Wife of the King (Nefertari Mery-en-Mut), justified'

identifying which king was the father of a 'King's Son' can prove very difficult. In a scene of a parade of royal children it has to be assumed that all the 'King's Sons' or 'Daughters' shown are offspring of the king who commissioned the scene. This may not always be the case. The royal harem was home to all the king's female relatives as well as his wives and children. A woman entitled 'King's Daughter' could have been the sister or cousin of the ruling monarch. The title indicates only that she was the child of a previous king. Unless a royal child became king or a 'Chief Royal Wife', the name given at birth was not enclosed in a cartouche. The full title which unequivocally gave the relationship between a prince and the king was 'King's Son, of His Body, Whom He Loves'. In addition to this a royal prince might also hold administrative, sacerdotal or military titles. Royal daughters rarely had titles other than that of 'Chantress' or 'Temple Singer'.

There are some examples of scenes of royal families in which each child is named. In the reign of Akehnaten the six princesses were often portrayed with their parents and each is very clearly identified as 'King's Daughter, of His Body, His Beloved, Born of the

25. Three of the daughters of Akhenaten shown accompanying their parents on an official occasion. In attendance is their aunt, Mutnedjmet. From the tomb of Ay at Amarna.

Translation (columns read from right to left):

1. King's daughter, of his body, his beloved, born to the King's Great Wife (Nefer-neferu-Aten Nefertiti), who lives forever and ever
2. King's daughter, of his body, his beloved . . .
3. Maket-Aten . . .
4. born of the King's Great Wife, his beloved . . .
5. (Nefer-neferuaten Nefertiti) etc . . .
6. King's daughter, of his body, his beloved, Ank-es-en-pa . . .
7. . . . Aten, born of etc . . .
8. . . . etc . . .
9. Sister of the King's Great Wife, Neferneferu-Aten Nefertiti
10. living forever and ever
11. Mut-nedjmet

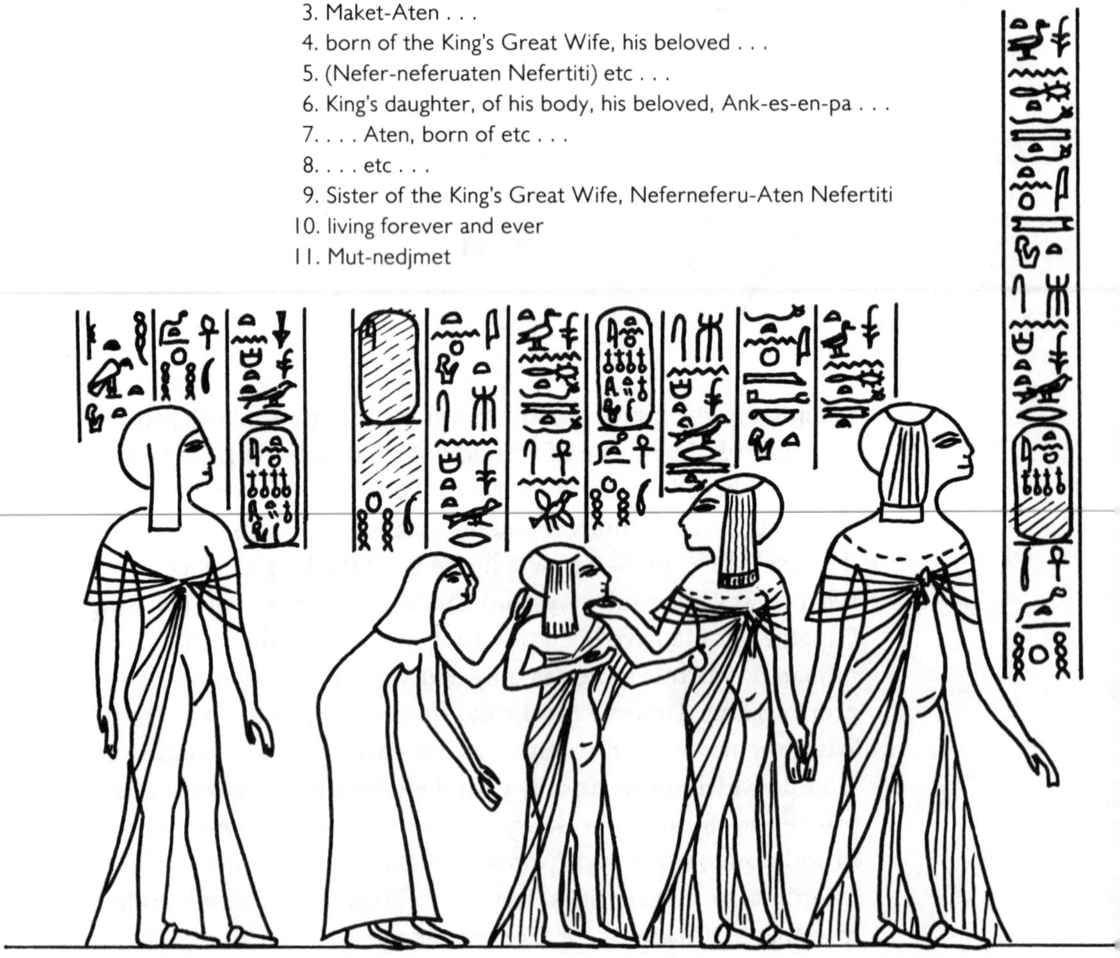

King's Chief Wife, Nefertiti'. The naming of both parents in this way is, however, rare (fig.25).

In the parades of children with which Ramesses II decorated his buildings at Luxor, the Ramesseum and Abu Simbel, among others, it is possible to identify by name more than one hundred sons and daughters. As they are shown in almost identical dress and of the same height, it is impossible to say which were the eldest, which were the children of Ramesses's successive 'Chief Wives' and which survived infancy. Some of the more senior princes are shown in scenes of the king's foreign campaigns taking part in battles, besieging a Canaanite fortress and driving their chariots. It is from the tombs and monuments of these princes that it is sometimes possible to identify their mothers. Ramesses was unusual in being married to two 'Chief Wives' at a time. Queen Isenofre was 'Great Royal Wife' at the same time as Queen Nefertari, and later in the king's reign of nearly sixty-eight years, the daughters of these two queens, Merytamen and Bint-Anath, became the consorts of their father in their mothers' places.

Ramesses III emulated Ramesses II in depicting his children on his monuments. His progeny were not as numerous as those of his hero though many sons bore the same names as the sons of the earlier king. In his mortuary temple of Medinet Habu several later kings sought to identify themselves in the parade of the children of Ramesses III by adding cartouches or the royal uraeus serpent at the brow to indicate kingship (fig.26).

It is not clear how regularly royal princesses were allowed to marry outside their own family. In the Sixth Dynasty the Vizier Mereruka was honoured by being given in marriage a 'King's Daughter' but she was very probably the child of a lesser wife or concubine rather than the daughter of the 'Chief Wife' of the reigning king (see fig.14, page 40). Princess Tia, daughter of Seti I, married a nobleman who became administrator of the Ramesseum. This marriage may have taken place before Seti became king so it cannot be taken as a typical example.

Although the king's family was probably just as badly affected by the high infant-mortality rate as the rest of the Egyptian population, there must have been many minor royal or semi-royal children

26. One of the sons of Ramesses III depicted at the mortuary temple of Medinet Habu. He wears the distinctive royal hairstyle of the elaborated sidelock and carries a single ostrich plume mounted on a baton, the badge of a 'Royal Fan-Bearer'.

Translation: Fan-bearer on the right of the king. His Majesty's First Charioteer, King's Son, of his body, Pa-Re-hir-wenam-ef, justified
Cartouche: Lord of Appearances, (Ramesses, Ruler of Iunw)

from several generations living at any one time. Those few who are known by name are known for very little else, but at least they are remembered and for that they would be grateful.

Table 5 gives hieroglyphic elements, particularly verbs, which occur frequently in the coronation (*nesu-bit*) names of the kings of Egypt. Abbreviations for wishes which often follow the names, such as joy, protection or dominion, are also included. The table is headed by the *nesu-bit* introduction, the sedge and the bee.

	tawy	The Two Lands		Heb Sed	Jubilee
	tawy	The Two Lands		Heb Sed	Jubilee
	sem	to unite		ka	spirit
	akh	to be useful		ba	soul, spirit
	wen	to exist, to be		shen	infinity
	di	to give, present, offer		djed	stability
	men	to establish		was	dominion
	in	to bring, fetch		sa	protection
	ii	to come		sa	protection
	is	to go		sekhem	power
	hotep	to satisfy, offer		aut-ib	joy
	aha	to fight		maet heru	True of Voice, Justified (deceased)

Table 5: Elements in Royal Names

4. SPIRITS OF PLACE

The king, as a god on earth, conferred a certain dignity on whichever city he chose as his principal residence. The court was peripatetic, visiting different cities at certain times of the year, particularly following the calendar of religious festivals. Though the administrative capital was usually established in the 'Residence City', there were branch offices of all government departments in other major towns; attached either to the palace or to the temple.

At the beginning of the First Dynasty a new royal capital was founded at the place which the Greeks called Memphis. The site was supposedly reclaimed in part from the Nile by damming and redirecting the river's flow, and its position at the apex of the Delta on the boundary between Upper and Lower Egypt was ideally suited to confirming the unified status of the Two Lands. The god of the region was Ptah, the creator who was known as the 'Greatest of Craftsmen'. The god's temple at the heart of the city was one of the first truly national shrines of Egypt, being founded at the very beginning of the dynastic era. The name of the temple was Hwt-ka-Ptah, 'Mansion of the Spirit of Ptah', which was used by the Greeks as a name for the whole city. Foreigners, having difficulty with the Egyptian pronunciations, corrupted this name to the Greek-sounding *Aiguptos* which, when applied to the country itself, gave rise to the modern name Egypt.

The ancient Egyptians had several names for their own country. 'Ta-mery', 'the Beloved Land', aptly expresses the feeling the people had for their homeland. Egyptians hated the idea of having to live in a foreign country or, worse still, dying there. They felt great pity for foreigners who were, by definition, inferior in every way to the true natives of Kem, the 'Black Land', a name derived from the rich alluvial soil of the Nile Valley. In keeping with the idea of equilibrium, the 'Black Land' was balanced by the 'Red Land' the desert. The Egyptian word for the desert includes the flamingo hieroglyph which signifies the colour red. It is not impossible that the very word *deserta* entered the Latin language by way of Egyptian. It is easy to imagine a Roman traveller asking the name of the sandy wastes to the east and west of the fertile valley only to be told 'Deshert'.

Two plants, now sadly extinct in Egypt, were used as heraldic emblems of the North and South. The papyrus (*Cyperus papyrus*) which represented Lower Egypt, the Delta, has been reintroduced in recent years to provide the raw materials for a lucrative tourist trade. The flowering reed or flag which represented Upper Egypt can no longer be identified in the Nile Valley. It is traditionally shown with a red standard and a blue fall. Clumps of each plant were used as hieroglyphs for the Two Lands and the flowering sedge was also used to indicate 'south' or 'southern' while either the papyrus or a whip symbol could signify the 'north'. East and west were designated by standards which may have derived from ancient local emblems or fetishes. They were the same as used for 'left' and 'right' respectively. The Egyptians defined left and right as the two banks of the Nile when facing upstream. Of course, the only proper way for a river to flow was from south to north so the Egyptians called the Tigris and the Euphrates 'the rivers which flow backwards'. The symbols for the cardinal compass directions may be seen on the general map of Egypt at the front of this book. The Nebty, 'Two Ladies', the patron goddesses of the North and the South are also shown on this map.

The cult centres of the Nebty, which were accorded national religious status, were the city of Nekheb in the south and the city called Buto by the Greeks in the north. The vulture goddess Nekhebt, whose name means simply 'She of Nekheb', was also known as the 'White One', an allusion to her wearing of the White Crown of Upper Egypt (see fig.16, chapter 2). The ruined site of her principal shrine is in the modern city of el-Kab in which, as in many Egyptian place names, an echo of the ancient name remains. As befits a national site of religious significance, Nekhebt's temple was called the 'Great Shrine', a name often applied to the city itself.

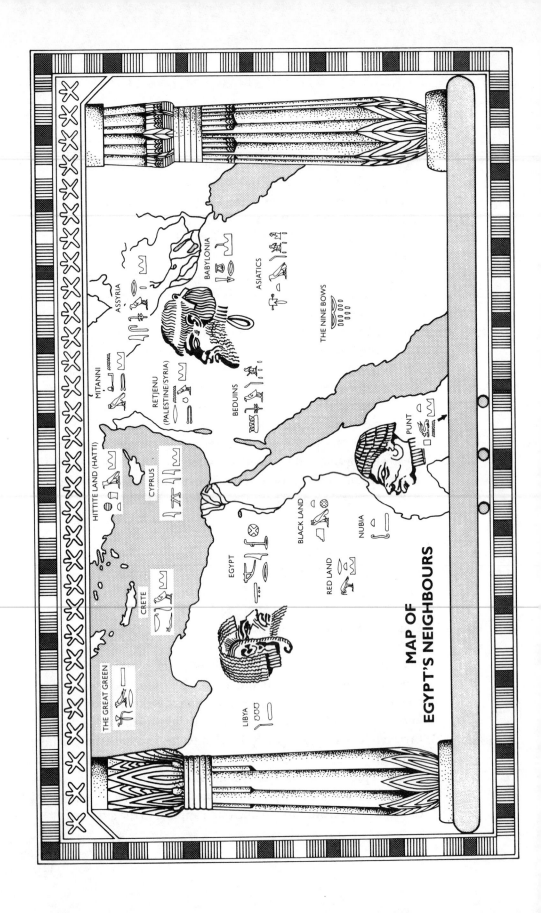

MAP OF
EGYPT'S NEIGHBOURS

Across the river from Nekheb was the city of Nekhen, which the Greeks called Hierakonpolis, 'Hawk Town'. This was one of the most ancient centres for the worship of the sky-god Horus who was represented as a falcon. The city in which the Horus temple stood was named after an even more ancient falcon deity who may be distinguished by the two tall plumes he wore as a crown. From earliest times Nekhen had been assimilated with the more generally accepted Horus who was worshipped at the temple as Har-Nekheny, Horus the Nekhenite. Throughout the country there were many shrines dedicated to Horus who was worshipped under various local titles. This practice is very similar to the Greek recognition of local variants of the cult of Apollo such as Delphic or Pythian Apollo. Nekhen was the spiritual heart of the south and a group of jackal-headed deities, known as the 'Souls of Nekhen', are thought to have represented the semi-mythical early rulers of the city.

The twin cities of Nekheb and Nekhen have northern counterparts in the towns of Pe and Dep which merged in ancient times to become the city known as Buto which itself is probably a Greek corruption of Pe-Dep. The cobra goddess of Lower Egypt, Wadjet, whose name means 'the Green One' or 'She of the Papyrus', was worshipped at the temple bearing her name, Per-Wadjet, the 'House of Wadjet', in the town of Dep. Pe is thought to have been the residence town of the earliest rulers of the Delta who are represented as falcon-headed deities known as the 'Souls of Pe'. In the second court at Medinet Habu, the Nebty and the 'Souls of Pe' and the 'Souls of Nekhen' are shown accompanying the king as he is presented to the Theban god Amen. In this scene it is interesting to note that Nekhebt, shown as a woman wearing the White Crown, is partnered by the 'Souls of Pe' while Wadjet, the 'Lady of the Red Crown', is followed by the 'Souls of Nekhen'. This is another indication of the unified state in which North and South were fully integrated. The remains of Buto are now called Tell el-Fara'an, the 'Mound of the Pharaohs'.

In Tables 6 and 7, pages 73 and 74, the hieroglyphic names of the towns numbered on the general map (page 6) are given with approximate pronunciations. Where a town had more than one name, as in the case of Memphis (9), only the first entry is numbered. Un-numbered entries refer to the site number last mentioned. By comparing them with the ancient Egyptian and the Classical place-names it is often possible to identify the origin of modern Arabic names. The site of Akhetaten, numbered (16), had no Classical equivalent since it was abandoned after the death of Akhenaten and was never rebuilt. The hieroglyphs at the head of each table represent the words 'places' and 'towns'.

The northern and southern lands were divided into provinces which are usually referred to as *nomes*, a Greek word. There were twenty-two Upper Egyptian and twenty Lower Egyptian nomes, each identified by its own standard. These emblems may have derived from symbols or fetishes associated with local deities and the name of a province may reflect the nature of the principal god of the region. The hieroglyph for '*nome*' or 'province' was a rectangular grid which represented a pattern of irrigation ditches and dykes. This symbol was used as the base on which the provincial emblems stood and in scenes of offerings from the regions each offering bearer may be identified by such a standard worn as a crown. Standards are seen being paraded before the king on the Narmer Palette, two of them bearing the emblem of a falcon and another the standing jackal of Wepwawet, the 'Opener of Ways'. This symbol is often represented preceding the king into battle and may be seen on the ivory label shown in figure 66 (page 178).

The Third Upper Egyptian province of which Nekhen was the capital was called the Shrine and its emblem was the double-feather crown of the Nekhenite. The First Lower Egyptian province, centred on Memphis, was called Ineb Hedj, the White Wall, a nickname for the city itself which must have had a distinctive white-washed or plastered surrounding wall. Two Lower Egyptian provinces, the Fourth and Fifth, had as their emblem the shield and crossed arrows of the warrior goddess Neith, patroness of the region. They were differentiated by the papyrus and sedge symbols representing north and south respectively. In Upper Egypt the Twentieth and Twenty-first *nomes* were both identified by the emblem of the sycamore tree, the Twentieth *nome* being described as *khenty* or 'foremost' while the Twenty-first was *pehwy* or 'behind'.

	Ta Mery (Egypt)		north
	Ta Shemau (Upper Egypt)		south
	Ta Mehu (Lower Egypt)		east, left
	Kem (The Black Land)		west, right
	Deshert (The Red Land)		Hapy (The Nile)
	district, province		waterway, canal, lake
	place, house		place, seat
	town, city		town, quarter, vicinity
	mansion, estate, administrative area		wall, fortification
	monument		palace
1	Pe		Niwt Weret	4
	Dep		Tjaru
	Per Wadjet		Hwt Ib	5
2	Sau		Per Bastet	6
3	Djedu		Ikheru	7
	Per Wsir		Iwnw	8

Table 6: Place-Names 1

#		Name		Name
9		Ankh Tawy		Hwt Sekhem
		Ineb Hedj		Iwnet
		Men Nefer	?	Gennu (?)
10		Tep Ihu		Qubt
11		Per Sebek		Waset
12		Er-Heny		Nesut Tawy
13		Nesen		Iwny Montju
14		Per Medjed		Qaay
15		Per Khmunu		Iwnyt
16		Akhet Aten		Nekhen
17		Qis		Nekheb
18		Sawty		Per Wer
19		Khent Min		Behdet
20		Hwt Repyt		Mesen
21		Tjeni		Nubet
22		Abdu		Suwan

Table 7: Place-Names 2

These could best be translated as Upper and Lower Sycamore Provinces. To the ancient Egyptians south took precedence over north and right over left. The maps which follow (Provinces of Upper and Lower Egypt) show the approximate locations of the ancient provinces of Upper and Lower Egypt together with their names and the standards by which they were represented. Many such provincial emblems may be identified in the inscriptions around the outer walls of the way-station or kiosk of Senusert I which is one of the most impressive exhibits in the Open Air Museum at Karnak.

The Fourth province of Upper Egypt was known as the Sceptre and its emblem was a decorated version of the sceptre which was the hieroglyph for 'dominion'. The city at the heart of this province was called Waset, 'the Sceptre' or even 'the Dominator', personified by a war-like goddess with the *was* sceptre as her headdress. Waset, sometimes called simply 'the City', was glorified in a poetical work dating from the Nineteenth Dynasty: 'Waset is the pattern for every city. . . All cities are founded in her true name since all are called 'City' after the example of Waset.'

This is the city which the Greeks called Thebes. As the seat of Amen-Re, King of the Gods, the city is also called 'Thrones of the Two Lands', one of the titles of the Karnak Temple. Another name given to Thebes was Iwnu Shema, the Southern Pillar. Iwnu was the name of the major cult centre of the sun-god Re, Heliopolis to the Greeks, which is rendered as On in the Bible. Several towns had the element iwn, meaning 'pillar' or 'column' in their names, like Iwnet (Denderah), Iwnyt (Esna) and Iwny (Armant). Since a column was the main support of a building, so it was seen as the central feature of a town, like a market cross or war memorial in an English town. The apparent repetition of such names for Egyptian towns is no more unusual than the proliferation of names like Newtown, Newham, Newton and Newborough in Britain, Villeneuve in France or Neuburg in Germany. All of these place-names have basically the same meaning. The original pillar had most probably disappeared at a very early stage from most Egyptian towns in whose names its symbol occurred. An analogy might be the persistence of the

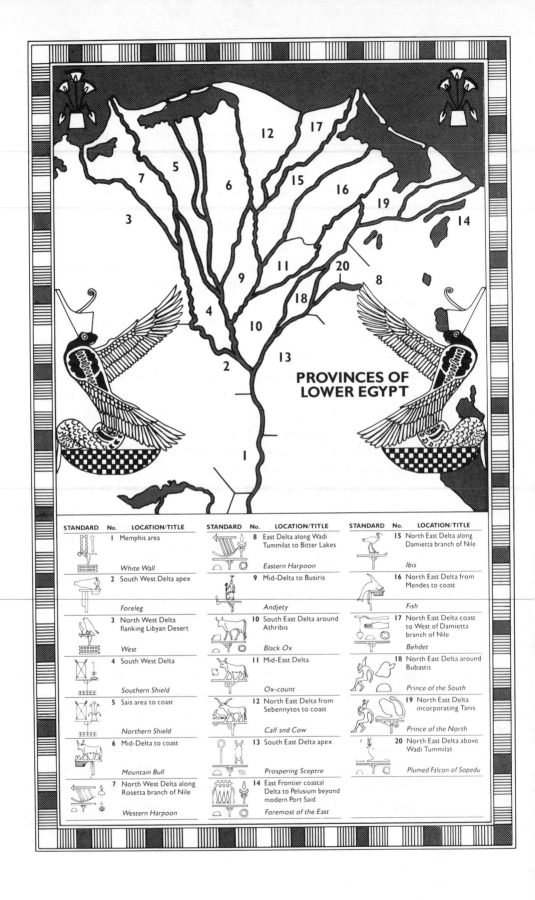

PROVINCES OF
LOWER EGYPT

STANDARD	No.	LOCATION/TITLE
	1	Memphis area
		White Wall
	2	South West Delta apex
		Foreleg
	3	North West Delta flanking Libyan Desert
		West
	4	South West Delta
		Southern Shield
	5	Sais area to coast
		Northern Shield
	6	Mid-Delta to coast
		Mountain Bull
	7	North West Delta along Rosetta branch of Nile
		Western Harpoon

STANDARD	No.	LOCATION/TITLE
	8	East Delta along Wadi Tummilat to Bitter Lakes
		Eastern Harpoon
	9	Mid-Delta to Busiris
		Andjety
	10	South East Delta around Athribis
		Black Ox
	11	Mid-East Delta
		Ox-count
	12	North East Delta from Sebennytos to coast
		Calf and Cow
	13	South East Delta apex
		Prospering Sceptre
	14	East Frontier coastal Delta to Pelusium beyond modern Port Said
		Foremost of the East

STANDARD	No.	LOCATION/TITLE
	15	North East Delta along Damietta branch of Nile
		Ibis
	16	North East Delta from Mendes to coast
		Fish
	17	North East Delta coast to West of Damietta branch of Nile
		Behdet
	18	North East Delta around Bubastis
		Prince of the South
	19	North East Delta incorporating Tanis
		Prince of the North
	20	North East Delta above Wadi Tummilat
		Plumed Falcon of Sopedu

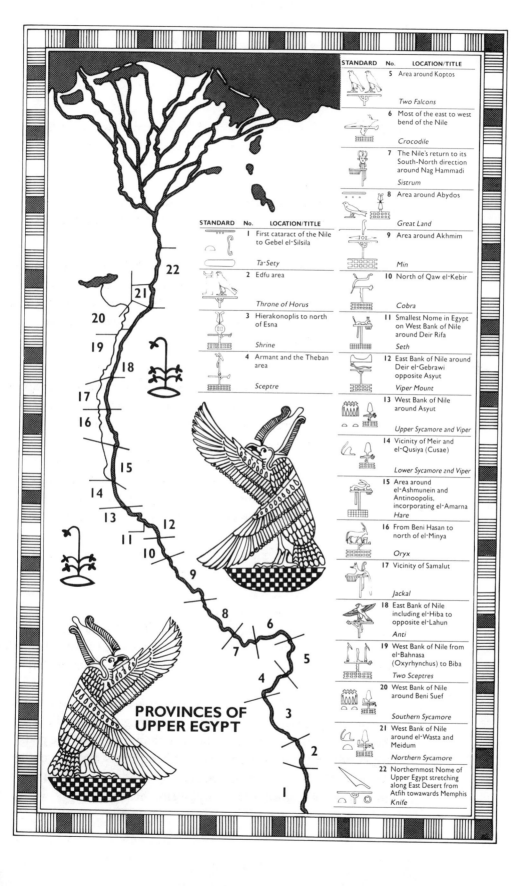

PROVINCES OF UPPER EGYPT

STANDARD	No.	LOCATION/TITLE
	1	First cataract of the Nile to Gebel el-Silsila
		Ta-Sety
	2	Edfu area
		Throne of Horus
	3	Hierakonoplis to north of Esna
		Shrine
	4	Armant and the Theban area
		Sceptre
	5	Area around Koptos
		Two Falcons
	6	Most of the east to west bend of the Nile
		Crocodile
	7	The Nile's return to its South-North direction around Nag Hammadi
		Sistrum
	8	Area around Abydos
		Great Land
	9	Area around Akhmim
		Min
	10	North of Qaw el-Kebir
		Cobra
	11	Smallest Nome in Egypt on West Bank of Nile around Deir Rifa
		Seth
	12	East Bank of Nile around Deir el-Gebrawi opposite Asyut
		Viper Mount
	13	West Bank of Nile around Asyut
		Upper Sycamore and Viper
	14	Vicinity of Meir and el-Qusiya (Cusae)
		Lower Sycamore and Viper
	15	Area around el-Ashmunein and Antinoopolis, incorporating el-Amarna
		Hare
	16	From Beni Hasan to north of el-Minya
		Oryx
	17	Vicinity of Samalut
		Jackal
	18	East Bank of Nile including el-Hiba to opposite el-Lahun
		Anti
	19	West Bank of Nile from el-Bahnasa (Oxyrhynchus) to Biba
		Two Sceptres
	20	West Bank of Nile around Beni Suef
		Southern Sycamore
	21	West Bank of Nile around el-Wasta and Meidum
		Northern Sycamore
	22	Northernmost Nome of Upper Egypt stretching along East Desert from Atfih towards Memphis
		Knife

suffix 'chester' or 'caster' in British place-names which indicates that they were the location of a *castra*, a Roman camp or fortification, most of which have been buried for centuries under subsequent buildings.

In the poem to Thebes, the importance of the three religious centres of Heliopolis, Memphis and Thebes itself is stressed in terms of their resident deities:

> All the gods are but three, Amen, Re and Ptah and there is none like them. Hidden is he named as Amen, Re is part of him as his face and Ptah is his body. Their cities abide eternally upon earth, Thebes, Heliopolis and Memphis forever. There is only he; Amen, Re and Ptah are three together in one.

Very little of the city of Heliopolis remains since it is largely hidden beneath the sprawling suburbs of Cairo. It was at Heliopolis that the first mound was thought to have arisen from the waters of chaos. The *bennu* bird, a heron with two streaming head plumes, was thought to have landed on this mound, known as the *ben-ben* and by its call to have summoned forth light to illumine the void. The child Re was born in the bud of a waterlily which appeared from the water and opened to reveal the god's head. When Re saw the newly created universe he wept for joy and his tears became men and women, the first Egyptians. The Temple of Re was thought to have been built on the very site of this 'First Occasion' and the cult symbol of the god was a pyramid-topped stone in imitation of the *ben-ben*. Perhaps it was this, or the first obelisk erected in honour of Re, which gave the city its Egyptian name.

The sun-god was worshipped at Heliopolis as the head of a family of nine deities, called the 'Great Ennead'. This word derives from the Greek meaning a 'group of nine'. Re, who is often linked with the elderly solar deity Atum as Re-Atum, was the self-created creator. His children Shu, god of the air, and Tefenet, goddess of moisture, were the parents of Geb, god of the earth, and Nut, goddess of the sky. The Ennead was completed by the four children of Nut, the gods Osiris and Seth, and their sisters Isis and Nephthys. Because of the nature ascribed to Seth, his place in the Ennead, especially in a funerary context, is often taken by Horus, the son of Isis.

Apart from the names already mentioned, the city of Ptah was known as Ankh Tawy, 'Life of the Two Lands', and the god's consort, the lioness-headed Sakhmet, was called 'Mistress of Ankh Tawy'. This confirms the importance of Memphis throughout Egyptian history, due as much to its strategic position as to its traditional role as Egypt's first capital. The kings of the Old Kingdom all appear to have ruled from Memphis and had their pyramid tombs built in the necropolis which spread north and south of the city on the west bank of the Nile. The southernmost of the Saqqara pyramids was built by Pepi I of the Sixth Dynasty. The town in which the pyramid builders lived and which the personnel employed in the king's mortuary cult continued to live after his death, was given the same name as the pyramid itself, Mennefer, 'Established and Beautiful'. This gave rise to its Greek name, Memphis, which became the name for the whole city whereas, originally, it had only applied to the southernmost suburb. A pyramid with its temple and complex of subsidiary buildings constituted a small town in its own right and each had its own name.

Pyramids were rarely inscribed, though mention of their names may be found in inscriptions in the reliefs decorating their satellite buildings or in the tombs of the priests and administrative officials employed there (see fig.47, page 134). The map on page 80 shows the locations of the principal pyramid sites. The names of the builders of these pyramids are listed on the map. The names given to the pyramids, both ancient and modern, where known, are presented in table 8.

The statues found in the Valley Temple of the third of the Giza Pyramids, built by King Menkaure, represent the king in the company of the goddess Hathor. In the case of triad groups, the third figure is that of a deity representing one of the regions in which there was an important Hathor shrine. Each deity, a true spirit of place, is identified by the standard which is worn as a headdress. Hathor was an extremely popular deity, the consort of Horus at his prime cult centre of Edfu, and Lady of Denderah, the modern name for the city which the Greeks called Tentyris. One of Hathor's titles was 'Lady of the Sycamore', (see fig.14, page 40).

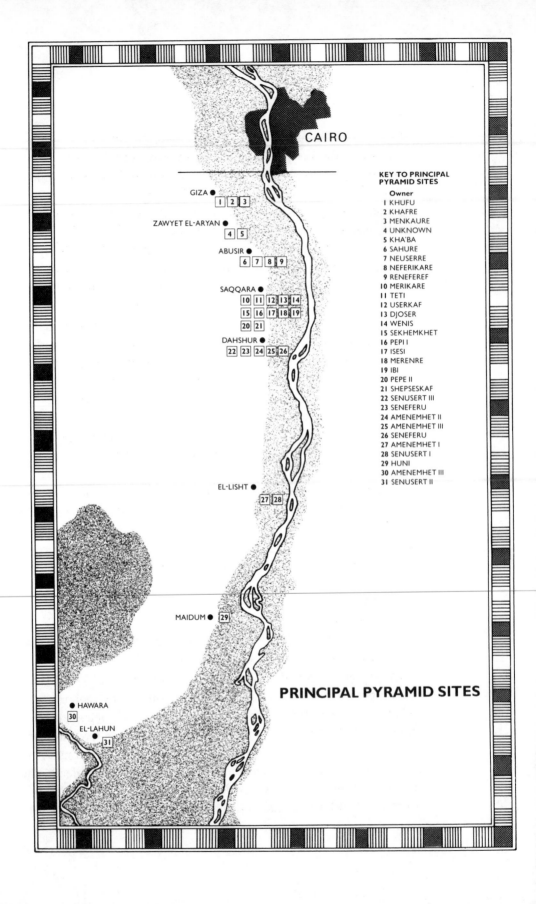

CAIRO

**KEY TO PRINCIPAL
PYRAMID SITES**

Owner
1 KHUFU
2 KHAFRE
3 MENKAURE
4 UNKNOWN
5 KHA'BA
6 SAHURE
7 NEUSERRE
8 NEFERIKARE
9 RENEFEREF
10 MERIKARE
11 TETI
12 USERKAF
13 DJOSER
14 WENIS
15 SEKHEMKHET
16 PEPI I
17 ISESI
18 MERENRE
19 IBI
20 PEPE II
21 SHEPSESKAF
22 SENUSERT III
23 SENEFERU
24 AMENEMHET II
25 AMENEMHET III
26 SENEFERU
27 AMENEMHET I
28 SENUSERT I
29 HUNI
30 AMENEMHET III
31 SENUSERT II

GIZA ● 1 2 3

ZAWYET EL-ARYAN ● 4 5

ABUSIR ● 6 7 8 9

SAQQARA ● 10 11 12 13 14
15 16 17 18 19
20 21

DAHSHUR ● 22 23 24 25 26

EL-LISHT ● 27 28

MAIDUM ● 29

PRINCIPAL PYRAMID SITES

● HAWARA
30
EL-LAHUN
31

#	Name		#	Name	
1	**Great Pyramid of Giza; Pyramid of Cheops** Where the sun rises and sets		17	The Beautiful	
2	**Second Pyramid of Giza; Pyramid of Chephren** The Great		18	Shining and Beautiful	
3	**Third Pyramid of Giza; Pyramid of Mycerinos** The Divine		19		
4	**Unfinished Pyramid**		20	Established and Living	
5	**Layer Pyramid**		21	**Mastabat el-Fara'un** The Purified	
6	Shining as the Ba-spirit		22		
7	Established of Places		23	**The Red Pyramid; The Northern Pyramid** The Shining	
8	Of the Ba-spirit		24	**The White Pyramid** The Mighty	
9	Divine as the Ba-spirits		25	**The Black Pyramid**	
			26	**The Bent Pyramid** The Southern Shining	
10	Flourishing of Places		27	High and Beautiful, or Places Appearing in Glory	
11	Enduring of Places				
12	Pure of Places		28	Favoured of Places, or Overlooking the Two Lands	
13	**Step Pyramid**				
14	Beautiful of Places		29	**The Maidum Pyramid**	
15	**Buried Pyramid**		30	**The Hawara Pyramid**	
16	Established and Beautiful		31	**The el-Lahun Pyramid** The Shining (?)	

Table 8: *Key to Pyramid Sites as numbered on Map. (Modern names shown in bold)*

27. From the tomb of Horemheb in the 'Valley of Kings'. The King stands before Hathor who is identified by the horned sun's disc worn as a crown, the same headdress as worn by Isis.

Translation (two columns above the king, left to right). The Osiris King (Djeser-kheperu-Re Setep-en-Re). Son of Re (Hor-em-heb Mery-en-Amen)
Goddess (reading right to left): For recitation by Hathor, Chieftainess of the West, Mistress of All the Gods, Lady of Heaven

She was seen as the guardian of the tree which offered shade and refreshment to the deceased as they journeyed from this world to the next. The tree was an important emblem of the goddess, especially in her role as a funerary deity in which she was called 'Chieftainess of the West'. The kingdom of the dead was called the 'Land of the Western Ones' because the entry to the underworld was thought to be on the western horizon, where the sun sets. Hathor was a cow-goddess of very ancient origin. She was depicted on the column capitals in her shrines as a woman with the ears of a cow and a crown formed of a cow's horns supporting the sun's disc (fig.27).

This same crown was later adopted by Isis and without being able to read their names, it is often difficult to tell the two goddesses apart. As 'Mistress of Heaven', Hathor was seen as the 'Celestial Cow' whose four legs were the supports of the vault of heaven and whose star-spangled belly was the sky itself. She was a mother-goddess who was particularly closely associated with the king. At Deir el-Bahri, the mortuary temple of Hatshepsut, Hathor is shown as the heavenly cow suckling the pharaoh. She was also the goddess who protected women in pregnancy and childbirth.

As the daughter of the sun-god, Hathor was sometimes called the 'Eye of Re', an avenging deity in the form of a lioness, also identified as Sakhmet, who was sent to punish mankind when they began to drift away from the true worship of the god. When he thought that his people had suffered enough, Re recalled his daughter but her condoned slaughter of humankind had given her a taste for blood and she refused to return. Re ordered a vast quantity of beer to be brewed which was then coloured with red ochre. This was poured over the fields where Hathor-Sakhmet was sleeping after one of her days of carnage. On waking and seeing the reddened beer and believing it to be human blood, the goddess drank herself into a stupor and then, suffering from what must have been the hangover to beat all hangovers, she swore she would never stray again. In order that mankind should not forget their narrow escape from annihilation, Re ordered that the event should be commemorated each year with a beer festival held in Hathor's honour. This was one of the most popular of all Egyptian religious festivals and was celebrated at New Year at all Hathor's shrines throughout the country, but primarily at Denderah which was consequently known as the 'Place of Intoxication'. Hathor herself was called the 'Lady of Drunkenness'.

Hathor was the principal deity worshipped at the two cities which the Greeks called Aphroditopolis since she was identified with the Greek goddess of love. These cities are now called Atfih, in the northernmost province of Upper Egypt, and Gebelein, in the south. In the latter, the temple of Hathor, Per-Hathor, gave rise to the alternative Greek name for the town, Pathyris. The town's ancient name, Kaay, means 'the Two Hills' or 'Twin Peaks' which is exactly the meaning of its modern Arabic name. At Hiw, to the west of Denderah, there was another Hathor shrine which had been dedicated originally to the even more ancient cow-goddess Bat, whose head decorated the sacred rattle or sistrum used in religious ritual.

At Edfu, Hathor is recognized as the wife of Horus. Her name means 'Mansion of Horus', indicating her position as a sky-goddess and protector or supporter of Horus the sky-god whose right eye was the sun and whose left eye was the moon. The province of which Edfu was the capital was called the 'Throne of Horus' and the temple which can be seen there today is the latest of a long line of shrines dedicated to the falcon god. He was revered there as the 'Falcon of Behdet', the winged sun's disc which was often used to decorate the lintel of a gateway or the curved top of a stela (see General Map, page 6).

The god was also known as Horus of Mesen, 'the Harpooner', who is shown in a series of reliefs along the outer walls of the central block of the temple at Edfu. These scenes show Horus defeating his enemy Seth, who is represented as a hippopotamus of insignificant size, by means of spearing the beast with a harpoon. Each blow of the weapon is guided by Isis, the mother of Horus, who is thus shown in her role as 'Mother of the God'. The child born to Hathor of her union with Horus was named Harsomtus by the Greeks. His Egyptian name, Har Sem-Tawy, means 'Horus the Uniter of the Two Lands'.

The family was the basic social unit in ancient Egypt and it was thought that the only proper way for people or gods to exist was within a family group. Each temple was seen as the home of a triad of deities, representing the unit family of husband, wife and child. There were very few complications within the relationships of Egyptian deities and no myths concerning divine infidelity or jealousy. The battles between Horus and Seth, and the part played in them by Isis, were largely a matter of contesting and defending the rights of Horus to his father's throne. There are no stories of a god becoming enamoured of a mortal though both Hatshepsut and Amenhotep III claimed to have been conceived of a union of the god Amen with the king's 'Chief Wife'. These claims were more political expedients than statements of real belief, intended to confer an air of both divine and royal legitimacy upon the two rulers. Most divine family groups were constant, and though there are examples of a god having different wives at different cult centres, there is no single temple where a bigamous relationship is celebrated. This reflects the nature of ancient Egyptian society which was essentially monogamous.

At Kom Ombo both Hathor and Horus were worshipped but not as husband and wife. The temple at the city which the Egyptians called 'Gold Town' is unique in being dedicated to two triads. It has two gateways, two halls and two sanctuaries. The northern part of the temple was dedicated to Horus who is partnered by a goddess named simply the 'Good Wife'. She was clearly an invention to provide Horus with a consort just as their child, with the artificial name 'Lord of the Two Lands', was created to complete the family. The southern part of the temple is dedicated to the premier deity of the shrine, the crocodile-god Sebek, son of the warrior-goddess Neith. His principal cult centre was at Medinet el-Fayum near the lake which the Greeks called Moeris from its Egyptian name Mer Wer, literally the 'Great Lake'. Crocodiles must have been particularly common in this region as at Kom Ombo, though Sebek's popularity in the country as a whole shows that his cult animal was widespread throughout the Nile Valley. The city built around his Fayum shrine took the name of the temple, Per-Sebek, and the Greeks called it, not unnaturally, Crocodilopolis. Sebek's consort at Kom Ombo was Hathor and the child who completed the divine family was the moon-god Khonsu. This is another artificial group since Khonsu is more usually associated with the Theban gods.

The symbol for 'god' was a primitive flag, a strip of cloth wrapped around a pole with the square-cut end flapping free at the top. The same sign was used to denote the adjective 'divine' and it is usually transcribed as netjer. The word 'goddess' was written either as the netjer symbol with the addition of the feminine 't' ending, or as a coiled and rearing serpent. On the Rosetta Stone the expression 'gods and goddesses' is rendered by the alternating netjer and serpent signs. Each sign is repeated three times this being the way in which the plural was denoted in hieroglyphs. This sign group is shown at the top of Tables 9 and 10 which give the most commonly used names and titles of Egypt's principal deities.

	Re		Iset (Isis)
	Re-Harakhty		Mother of the God
	Atum		Goddess in her many names
	Khepri		Nebet Hwt (Nephthys)
	Aten		Set, Sutekh (Seth)
	Har-Wer (Haroeris)		Inpu (Anubis)
	Shu (air)		who is in the sacred booth
	Tefenet (moisture)		who is in the place of embalming
	Geb (earth)		Lord of the Necropolis
	Nut (sky)		who is on his mountain
	The Mysterious		Har (Horus)
	Wsir (Osiris)		the Child (Harpocrates)
	Foremost of the Westerners		Son of Isis (Harsiese)
	who is in Andjety		Pillar of his Mother
	who is in Heliopolis		Saviour of his Father
	Foremost of Rosetjau		First of the Womb

Table 9: Deities: Names and Titles 1

	Hwt-Har (Hathor)		Mut
	Chieftainess of the West		Khonsu
	Mistress of Heaven		Montju (Month)
	Lady of the Sycamore		Djehuti (Thoth)
	Mistress of Intoxication		Min
	Horus, Uniter of the Two Lands (Harsomtus)		Neith
	Ptah	or	Maet
	Beautiful Face		Daughter of Re
	Lord of Truth		Bastet
	Sakhmet		Wadjet
	Lady of Ankh Tawy		Nekhebt
or	Amen		The White One
	King of the Gods		Wosret
	Lord of Thrones	or	Khnum
	in the southern sanctuary (Luxor)	or	Sebek (Suchos)
	Bull of his Mother		Sokar

Table 10: Deities: Names and Titles 2

At the beginning of the Middle Kingdom, kings of the Eleventh Dynasty sprang from the Theban area and revered the war god Montu as shown by the given name Montuhotep which became very popular at that time. His cult centre was in the city known as Her-Montju, 'Under Montu', which the Greeks called Hermonthis and which is now known as Armant. This is one of the clearest survivals of an ancient place-name into modern usage. Montu was shown as a falcon-headed man. The Twelfth Dynasty originated in Thebes itself as is shown by the use of the personal name Amenemhet. Amen gradually usurped the position of Montu within the Thebaid to become the principal deity of the region and eventually the premier national god of Egypt.

Amen was not a native of the Theban area. His name means 'hidden', 'unseen' or 'invisible'. Originally he was one of the four gods who, with their female counterparts, formed the ogdoad (group of eight) worshipped at the town of Khmunu, a name with the rather prosaic meaning, 'Eight Town'. This expression is still obvious in the modern name Ashmunein. The principal god of the city was the moon-god and scribe Thoth. The 'Eight' were said to have created between them the 'Cosmic Egg' from which the universe was hatched. Amen's colleagues were Kuk ('darkness'), Heh ('infinity') and Nun ('primordial waters'). His consort was Amaunet, a feminine version of the god's name, and it was she who was first adopted as the goddess of the Middle Kingdom temple erected to Amen at Karnak. Montu was adopted into the Theban triad as the divine child. The statues dedicated by Tutankhamen show both Amen and Amaunet but by his time the goddess recognized as Amen's consort was Mut whose name, written with the vulture hieroglyph, means 'mother'. When used to represent the name of the goddess, the vulture has a flail-sceptre tucked behind her wing. Mut was shown as a woman wearing the 'Double Crown' or the 'Queen's Crown', as befitted her position as the 'Queen of the Gods'. At her own temple at Karnak she is also associated with Sakhmet and Hathor and is shown with the head of a lioness. At the Ramesseum, the mortuary temple of Ramesses II, Mut in her lioness form is shown presenting the king to her husband Amen.

Standing behind Amen's throne in the Ramesseum relief is the child of the couple, the moon-god Khonsu, who replaced Montu as the third member of the Theban triad. He is most often shown as a child wearing the shroud-like garment which is also associated with Ptah, his childishness indicated by the plaited 'Sidelock of Youth'. His hands hold regal sceptres and on his head he wears the lunar symbol of the crescent of the new moon with the disc of the full moon resting within it. According to a story told on a stela now in the Louvre, Khonsu had a reputation as a god of healing, with the ability to drive out evil spirits, which had spread even to foreign lands since the Prince of Bakhtan requested the King of Egypt send the healing statue of the god to his country to cure the desperately ill Princess Bentresh, sister of Pharaoh's own wife Neferure. Though written down as late as the fourth century BC this story seems to relate to the time of Ramesses II when the king married a princess of the Hittites who took the Egyptian name Maneferure.

The cult which was most universally accepted was that of Osiris. The god was worshipped at Heliopolis as one of the Great Ennead but it was in his role as a god of fertility and as the 'King of the Dead' that he appealed to all people, for everyone's life depended upon agriculture and everyone hoped to be reborn in the 'Land of the Western Ones'. One of Osiris's most commonly used titles was Khenty Imentiu, 'Foremost of the Westerners'. The legend of the murder of Osiris by his treacherous brother Seth, and his subsequent resurrection as 'Ruler of Eternity', is a classic myth-cycle which may be found in many cultures. According to a late version of the story, the god's body was ripped into fourteen parts (other stories give different numbers) each of which was buried in a different place giving rise to Osiris shrines throughout Egypt. The heart was thought to have been buried at Athribis in the Delta, hence its ancient name Hwt-Ib, 'Mansion of the Heart', and its modern name Tell Atrib. At Abusir, the classical Busiris, both of which names derive from the Egyptian Per-Wsir, 'House of Osiris', the backbone was said to have been buried. This was represented by the djed pillar used as the hieroglyph for 'stability', and the ancient name of the city was Djedu. Osiris was often called 'Lord of Djedu' as in the text which heads this chapter (page 68).

The most important and probably the most ancient shrine of Osiris was at Abydos, a Greek version of the ancient place-name, Abdu, where tradition held that the god's head had been buried. The fetish of Osiris used as the emblem of the *nome* of Abydos was said to represent the mummified head surmounted by two plumes. The province was also called 'the Great Land'. The temples built at Abydos by Seti I and Ramesses II were national shrines in every sense of the word. Though principally dedicated to Osiris, each had several subsidiary chapels for the other national deities – Re, Ptah and Amen – as well as the kings themselves. Osiris was thought to have been the first king of Egypt whose throne was inherited by Horus. Every king was Horus incarnate while he lived and became Osiris when he died.

Osiris was thought to have taught his people all about agriculture, crop-growing, the use of tools and viticulture. His principal festival at Abydos was the 'Feast of the Vintage', an October festival which celebrated the wine harvest. As part of this celebration a passion play was enacted retelling the story of the god's life, death and rebirth. As a god of fertility he had similarities with Amen in his procreative form as worshipped at the Luxor Temple, and with the ithyphallic fertility god Min of Coptos. All three gods may be shown with green or black skin representing vegetation or the fertile soil of Egypt. In tombs Osiris is shown as the king of the next world receiving the deceased into his kingdom once they have passed the test of 'Weighing the Heart'. The word 'Osiris' became synonymous with deceased and 'an Osiris' meant a dead person.

Anubis, the most important of the many gods shown with the head of a jackal, was recognized as guardian of the necropolis, hence his title 'Lord of the Sacred Land', and as the loyal nephew who had embalmed his uncle's body for burial. In his role as the undertaker of Osiris he was called 'Lord of the Place of Embalming' and 'he who is before the sacred booth', an expression which refers to the tented shrine erected before the tomb, in which the embalming rituals took place. Anubis is also called 'he who is on his mountain'. This title describes the appearance of the jackal on the skyline, prowling the western clifftops, as if patrolling the necropolis. The two sisters Isis and Nephthys are seen as mourners at the funerary

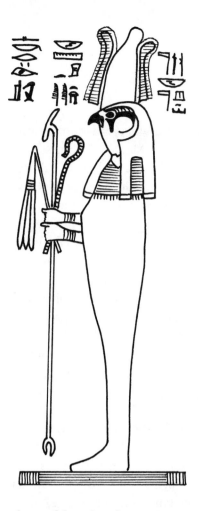

28. The funerary god Sokar. Closely associated with both Ptah and Osiris he wears the shroud-like garment common to both.

Translation (left to right): Sokar-Orisis, Lord of the Mysterious Region, the Great God, Lord of the Necropolis

bier of their brother Osiris, sometimes with feathered wings outspread to protect his body, and with two more goddesses, the warrior Neith and the scorpion Serqet, they were thought to guard the body for eternity and their figures were carved or painted at the four corners of the sarcophagus which held the king's coffin as may be seen in Tutankhamen's tomb.

Another god of the necropolis was the ancient falcon-god Sokar whose cult originated in the Memphis area (fig.28). From early times he was closely associated with the Memphite god Ptah and his name was usually written as the composite Ptah-Sokar. He is shown with the shrouded body of Ptah and the head of a hawk, and was worshipped at sanctuaries in the great necropolises of Lower Egypt as well as being linked with Ptah at Abydos. The position held by Sokar during the Old Kingdom as the premier funerary deity and god of the underworld was gradually assumed by Osiris so that in the Middle Kingdom, the deity became known as Ptah-Sokar-Osiris.

[91

The god's distinctive bark was paraded in the annual Festival of Sokar which is recorded at Medinet Habu. Sokar was almost certainly, in his earliest form, a god of agriculture like Osiris. He had also been recognized as the patron deity of craftsmen, a position usually associated with Ptah, and continued to be seen as the protector of goldsmiths.

Gold was mined in Egypt itself, but no further north than Coptos which was the town controlling the main caravan-routes through the eastern desert via the Wadi Hammamat and the Wadi el-Qash to the Red Sea. Many of the gold-bearing regions exploited by the Egyptians were in Nubian territory. The province, centred on Aswan where the First Cataract marked the southernmost boundary of Egypt, was given the same name as the country known now as Nubia. There were two principal Nubian tribal areas recognized as separate states in ancient times. The northernmost was called Wawat and to the south was Kush. These places were viewed in a rather ambiguous light by the ancient Egyptians. Nubian produce was regularly depicted in parades of offering bearers. Animal skins, hard woods such as ebony, incense, ivory, ostrich feathers and eggs, and gold were all claimed as tithe from the tributary territories. On the other hand, many kings found it necessary, at the start of a reign, to conduct a military expedition if not a full-scale war in Nubia to establish Egyptian authority. Nubian archers were welcomed into the Egyptian army and intermarried with the native population, yet several Nubian tribes were named among the 'Nine Bows', the traditional enemies of Egypt. These enemies were depicted as bound captives, sometimes with their names in cartouches replacing their bodies. In such examples, the outline of the 'cartouche' is shown as an embattled wall. (see fig.7, page 27). It is not clear what criteria were employed in choosing the traditional nine enemies though a 'set' usually included some Nubians, some Asiatics and at least one Libyan. Some examples of such a collection include very vague names like 'the Southland' or 'Nubian Land'. In the Eighteenth-Dynasty tomb of Aanen in the Theban hills, the list which decorates the dais on which Aanen's sister and brother-in-law, Queen Tiye and Amenhotep III, are seated, includes the Keftiu, identified as the Cretans, and the people of Mitanni, a kingdom which existed to the north of Syria and which the Egyptians also called Naharin (fig 29). Such named figures are always called the 'Nine Bows' even if, as in the case of Aanen's tomb, more than nine are depicted! Lists of military conquests were also shown in this way. At Karnak the Sixth Pylon is decorated with the anthropomorphized names of the cities, tribes and towns vanquished by Thutmose III in his campaigns. It is possible to identify several Biblical place-names among the Canaanite conquests.

29. Three bound captive figures from the tomb of Aanen at Thebes. Their distinctive clothes, hairstyles and facial features identify them as accurately as their names.

Translation (reading right to left): Naharin (Mitanni); Irem [a region of Nubia]; Keftiu [Crete].

The other foreign peoples with whom Egypt came into contact may be seen in the reliefs depicting the major campaigns of New Kingdom monarchs. Ramesses II had his conflict with the Hittite Confederacy shown at all his most important monuments such as Abu Simbel, Abydos and the Ramesseum. Merenptah recorded his successes against the Nubians and the Asiatic tribes of Canaan and Syria on the great stela, now in the Cairo Museum, which is called the Israel Stela because it bears the only mention of the tribe of Israel in all known Egyptian documents. At Medinet Habu the desperate conflicts between Ramesses III and the Libyans and the Peoples of the Sea are vividly portrayed (fig.30). The map of 'Egypt's Neighbours' (page 70), shows the names of the most important foreign peoples with whom Egypt had contact.

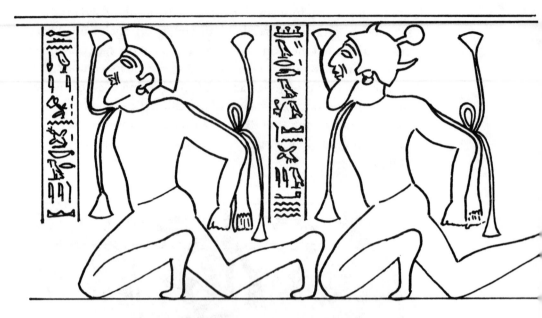

30. Token prisoners of war representing two of the Sea Peoples encountered by Ramesses III. From a relief at Medinet Habu.

Translation: Left: A chief of the enemy, the Tjekary (Tjeker)
Right: Shardana (Sherden) of the sea

This degree of international communication led to the establishment of Egyptian colonies and fortified outposts in foreign lands. There were ambassadors, city governors and military commanders appointed to care for Egyptian interests, and wherever the Egyptians went, their gods went too. The goddess Hathor was perhaps the most widely travelled. She was patroness of the turquoise mines in Sinai, as shown by her title 'Lady of the Turquoise'. She was also revered by the inhabitants of the southern incense land of Punt, the exact location of which has not been determined. In the north she was called 'Lady of Byblos', the coastal city in the Lebanon where Egyptian ships sailed to collect huge quantities of cedar and pinewood.

The Greeks tried to associate each of the principal Egyptian gods with deities from the Hellenistic pantheon. Thoth was called Hermes, Min became Pan and Ptah was Hephaestus. The Romans continued the assimilation and the worship of Amen in the form of

Jupiter-Ammon and that of the goddess Isis in her own right were exported to Rome. In fact, the mystery cult which surrounded the Roman devotion to Isis was extremely popular and many classical shrines were built to her including one at Pompeii, and another on the Acropolis itself. The worship of Isis survived longer than any other cult in Egypt, her temple at Philae being the last resort of Egyptian religious ritual to be taken over by Christianity.

There is no doubt that the ancient spirits of places in Egypt have outlived the majority of their believers by thousands of years since their names, albeit in forms somewhat different from the originals, are still in everyday use. Despite the changes in national religion from paganism to Christianity and finally to Islam, the gods of the ancient Egyptians are still remembered in the names of their shrines.

5. BE A SCRIBE

The development of writing in ancient Egypt may be traced from simple pot-marks in the pre-dynastic era, through the jar-sealings and labels of the period immediately after the 'Unification', to the appearance of more recognizably grammatical constructions in the late First Dynasty. These examples of writing show the evolution of the hieroglyphic script from what must have been purely pictorial origins to the sophisticated use of both ideograms and phonograms. In the course of the next 3000 years many signs changed in the way they were used or the sounds they represented, and many more were added to the working list available to the Egyptian scribe.

The origins of the Egyptian script are very vague. Trade and cultural connections with Mesopotamia at the dawn of Egypt's social development may have introduced the concept of writing to the people of the Nile Valley but the style of the script and the constructions used are apparently home-grown. There is a degree of similarity in the grammar of ancient Egyptian with that of other Semitic tongues, such as Aramaic and Hebrew, and yet there are also elements which connect it with the North African Hamitic languages. This is enough to indicate that the language itself evolved in situ and that the script used to write it was also a purely Egyptian invention. The Egyptians called hieroglyphs 'the God's Words' and considered them to be the creation of Thoth who is often shown in scenes of the 'Weighing of the Heart' making a written record of the judgement of the deceased (fig.31).

In the earliest periods the use of writing was very closely linked to the kingship. The king and his closest officials could demonstrate their authority by having their possessions and monuments labelled with their names. This implies that the upper echelons of society were, to some degree, literate, or at least that they had servants

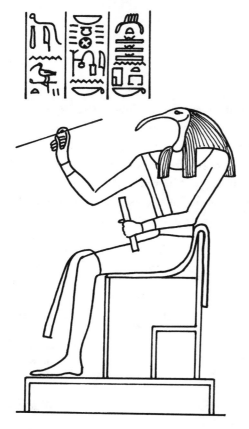

31. The god Thoth enthroned, from the temple of Ramesses II at Abydos.

Translation (columns read left to right): For recitation by Thoth, Lord of Khmunu (Hermopolis), the Scribe, '[may there be] to you joy in your mansion [temple]'

who could both read and write. There seems to have been an inbred need to record ownership and to keep records, not only of the king's achievements but also of the day-to-day business of the temples and palaces. Everything was committed to writing – inventories of store-rooms, reports from local officials, lists of building materials. In order to supply the very real need to have everything in writing, a class of scribes was essential. From the First Dynasty, and probably earlier, Egyptian society was bureaucratic and the valued position of the scribe in that society was assured.

A scribe's basic training in reading and writing was his most important asset. His most prized possession was his palette. The scribal palette was a narrow, rectangular piece of wood with a central longitudinal slot in which reed pens were kept, and two round depressions at one end which held blocks of black and red ink pigment. Elaborate versions of the palette may have had sliding or swivelling panels to hold the pens in place and some were inlaid with ivory or carved with at least the owner's name and sometimes also an invocation to the god Thoth, the patron of all scribes. Palettes with more than the two basic colours were essentially artists' paintboxes. There is one such, in the British Museum, which belonged to the Royal Steward Mery-Re of the Eighteenth Dynasty. This has no fewer than fourteen paint or pigment depressions.

Pens were made from reeds which were available in abundance throughout Egypt. The scribe chose a reed according to the width and coarseness of the writing tip he required, then he sucked or chewed the end of it to split the fibres so forming a crude brush.

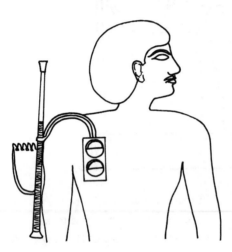

32. Hesy-Re, a highly favoured court official in the Third Dynasty. Among other titles he was 'Chief Scribe to the King'. He carries his scribe's equipment slung over his shoulder.

The ink was similar to modern poster paint. It was made from finely ground pigment – charcoal for black, ochre for red – mixed with a mild gum such as that obtained from acacia seeds, and shaped into cakes which were allowed to dry. The ink was taken up by moistening the reed brush with water and swirling it over the surface of the ink block. The method of writing was very similar to that of Japanese calligraphy. The scribe's hand did not rest on the writing surface and his strokes were smooth and fluent. When his pen became ragged or splayed he simply cut off the worn end and chewed the next section. When the pen became too short to use he threw it away and cut another reed. Of course, he would cut several reeds at once to save time, keeping only those in use in the palette pen-slot and storing his spares in a tubular pen-case which could be elaborately decorated to resemble a papyriform or palmiform column.

Other items of equipment such as a small bowl for water, a simple flint-blade for cutting and sharpening pens, spare blocks of ink and perhaps a scrap of soft leather and a piece of sandstone which were used as erasers, were kept in a drawstring bag. These three elements – palette, pen-case and bag – comprised the classic set of a scribe's equipment and became the hieroglyph for scribe and anything to do with writing (fig.32).

Even the highest official in the land was always conscious of the fact that he owed his position to his education and was happy to have himself portrayed as an ordinary scribe sitting cross-legged with his kilt held taut across his knees to form a simple desk,' and the scribe's equipment hanging from his shoulder. Hesyre who, among other titles, held that of 'Chief of the Royal Scribes' in the reign of King Djoser of the Third Dynasty, is portrayed in two delicately carved wooden panels from his tomb close to the Step Pyramid at Saqqara. In each portrait the scribe's palette, pen-case and bag are prominent. In the reign of Amenhotep III, the king's closest minister and architect, Amenhotep, son of Hapu, was granted the great honour of being allowed to set statues of himself within the sacred precincts of the Karnak Temple. In these statues he chose to be portrayed as a simple scribe with no overt indication of his prominent position at court. This is not an example of humility in the presence of the god, for the very fact that Amenhotep's having his statues placed in the temple was, for a commoner, a unique demonstration of his importance. The guise of scribe was a deliberate choice to emphasize the basis of his success. The statue of Horemheb, which is now in the Metropolitan Museum of Art in New York, shows him in his early years as an army scribe, his head bent studiously over the papyrus spread out on his lap.

Education was the key to success and no-one was barred from literacy because of superstition or the existence of a closed shop for scribes. Village scribes could take on apprentices to help with the business of letter-writing, drawing up labour contracts and other such mundane transactions. Local officials were always on the lookout for likely lads who showed an aptitude for learning and who could be trained for the civil service. There were schools attached to local administrative offices as well as the government

33. Two offering-bearers from a Theban tomb of the Eighteenth Dynasty. The name and titles of each are given.

Translation: Left: Head of the house of the Chancellor, the scribe, Nu
Right: Scribe of the Documents [clerk?] to the Chancellor, Sebek-hotep

departments in the principal towns. The Egyptian governmental machine depended on a vast army of clerks, taxation officers, recorders and accountants (fig.33).

In theory even the lowliest peasant boy, if he showed talent, could aspire to an education as long as he could bring himself to the notice of someone who was in a position to help him. No matter what sacrifices were required to keep him during his training he would be spared from work in the fields because having a scribe in the family was a great mark of status.

There were many highly placed court officials who were proud to proclaim their humble origins. Senenmut, chief advisor and architect to Queen Hatshepsut, rose to the heights of society from a very ordinary Theban family. The already-mentioned Horemheb went even further. He became King's Secretary, Commander-in-Chief of the Army, King's Deputy and finally King in his own right. He lived through the reigns of at least four other kings before successfully ruling Egypt himself for more than a quarter of a century.

The sons of upper-middle-class families and the nobility were almost expected to be literate. They might well have had private tutors and the sons of court officials could have been educated with the royal princes who had access to the best and wisest of teachers. The larger temples supported scribe schools where boys entered into training from as young as five years of age.

The written language was taught in its hieratic form. This was a short-hand version of hieroglyphs which had been used in parallel with the more decorative script from earliest times. It took up less space than hieroglyphs and was quicker to write. Hieratic could be written, like hieroglyphs, in columns or rows but was always read from right to left like Arabic. Most everyday documents such as contracts, wills, letters and inventories were written in hieratic so it was that script which the student scribe was set to learn from the start of his education.

At first he would practise writing the different signs, learning how they fitted together in lines or columns and how they could be combined to form composite signs. Each scribe developed his own distinctive handwriting so that often modern Egyptologists can identify the name of the scribe who penned a document just by looking at it. A student was called a *seba*, a word derived from the verb 'to teach'. Apparently the word had the same sound as the word for 'star' since the principal sign employed in it was the star hieroglyph. A teacher was *sebai* and the word for instruction, education in general and learning or wisdom was *sebayt*. A personal tutor bore the masculine form of the title 'nurse'. Several tutors of the royal princes are known from autobiographical details in their tombs. One such was the father of Paheri of el-Kab. His name, It-rw-renpi, translates as 'Father of the Young Lion'. 'Father' was a word which could have been used as a term of endearment by a pupil for his tutor. The 'Young Lion' could have been a euphemism for 'Prince', the prince in question being the 'King's Son' Wadjmose who is shown with his brother Amenmose in the same tomb. Is it possible that this name is in fact a pseudonymous nickname which was used in preference to the man's given name?

Exercises in the setting out and composition of letters took up much of a student's lesson time. It was important that he learned the correct modes of address and he spent many hours copying model letters, both real and fictitious, of the sorts he might be called upon to write when he took up his career in earnest. Copying was the prime method by which the student learned. Texts were written on a whitewashed board which was hung on the schoolroom wall for the students to copy. These copy boards and the copies made by the students may be found in many museums.

The texts employed were not always letters. Extracts from stories considered 'classics' by the Egyptians and works known as 'Wisdom Literature' were often used, presumably to keep the interest of the boys who had to copy them. The student's work would be corrected in red ink by his tutor. In many instances modern knowledge of certain Egyptian literary works is based wholly on such student copies, grammatical errors and spelling mistakes included. The work was most commonly done on ostraca, flakes of stone which were easy to obtain from the debris generated by building works such as the excavation of tombs in the limestone cliffs. Ostraca, being cheap and available, were rarely reused. They were the ancient equivalent of scrap paper or memo pads. They are also durable and texts written on stone flakes have survived while those written on leather rolls or papyrus, which were the materials used for more important works, have not. Papyrus was too valuable to be wasted on the everyday work of mere students, though they would have had opportunities to become acquainted with its production and use as part of their training.

The most common form of copy material provided for students was moralistic, giving advice as to acceptable behaviour at the same time as acquainting the copyist with grammatical construction. It was hoped that the student would learn the moral as he copied the text. The authors of these texts used several themes in their attempts to persuade the student to dedicate himself to his studies.

34. A member of the staff of Maya, the Treasury Minister at the end of the Eighteenth Dynasty. From Maya's Memphite tomb.

Translation: The Treasury Scribe, Sen-nefer, justified

The writers often made comparisons between the life of the scribe and those of other tradesmen:

> Do you not consider how badly things fare for the farmer when his harvest is registered? Pests have taken half the corn. Mice infest the field and locusts have descended. Cattle devour and sparrows steal. Thieves take what is left from the threshing floor. Woe to the farmer! . . . When the scribe arrives at the riverbank to register the harvest, bringing with him the porters carrying their sticks, they say, 'Give over the corn!' The farmer says, 'There is none'. He is stretched out and beaten; he is bound and thrown into a ditch. But as for the scribe, he directs the work of all people. For him there are no taxes because he pays his tribute in writing; there are no dues for him. Take heed of this!

Similar texts dealing with the life of a soldier, a baker and a gardener, among others, are all exaggerated in the same way to make the scribe's lot seem enviable.

Reports on the student's progress were made regularly to his parents or sponsors. Some of the most frequently copied texts purport to be letters from home in response to unfavourable reports, an obvious attempt to shame the student into hard work:

> Do not be idle, do not waste your time, or you will be soundly beaten. Do not give yourself over to pleasures, that will be your ruin. Write with your hand, read with your mouth and seek advice from those who are wiser than you. Aspire to the profession of magistrate, make this your goal as you grow older. A scribe that is skilled in his calling, a master of education, is most fortunate. Persevere every day to obtain the mastery of writing. Spend not a moment in idleness or you will be beaten. A boy's ear is on his back; he only hears when he is beaten. Take these words to heart for your own good.

Another text shows that the strict discipline referred to above was nothing as to that experienced by a father who, in his day, had also trained as a scribe:

> Think how it was with me when I was your age. I passed my time

with my limbs bound. I was virtually a prisoner in the temple for three months while my parents and my brothers worked the land. When my bonds were removed and my hands were free then I did better than anyone had ever done before.
I was top of my class, surpassing all of my comrades in book learning. Do as I say and you will be successful. You will be found at the end of the day to have no superior.

Problems of youthful high spirits and drunkenness associated with students seem to be nothing new:

I am told you are neglecting your studies, giving yourself over to pleasures. You go from street to street in that part of the town where it stinks to high heaven of beer. You are found climbing a wall and breaking down a door. Men run away from you because you would pick a fight with them. I wish you would understand that wine is an abomination. I wish you would take the pledge, that you would turn away from beer and forget wine. You are found sitting in a house surrounded by girls, with flowers around your neck. You pat your beer-belly and fall on your face in the mud.

Certain classic books categorized as 'Wisdom Literature' were also used as copy material. A book supposedly written by Ptah-hotep, the Vizier of the Fifth-Dynasty King Isesi, was a very popular moralistic work: Do not become arrogant because of your knowledge and do not think you know everything. Take advice from the ignorant as well as from the wise, for you can never know all there is to know. No artist is ever a complete master of his skill.

A similar work known as the Instruction of Duauf was probably written specifically as a school textbook. The author writes as if he was a father giving advice to his son whom he was accompanying to the capital in order to enrol him in the 'House of Documents' to train as a scribe. The whole text is a marvellous public-relations exercise on behalf of schools and education, using the recognized techniques of comparing professions and exhorting the student to make the most of his education: 'What I am now telling you in this voyage to the capital I say for love of you. Every day spent in school will be profitable to you. Its work will endure like mountains.'

Some of the surviving student copies of the Instruction of Duauf are so corrupt and riddled with mistakes that they are unintelligible. Clearly the method of teaching by setting copywork was not immediately successful.

Once the hieratic script had been learned to a proficient standard, the student would begin to learn hieroglyphs. A papyrus roll found at Tanis in the Delta proved to be a sort of dictionary of hieroglyphs which might have been a scribe's reference book of the sort used in scribe schools. It consists of columns of hieroglyphs, each with its hieratic equivalent and a few words in hieratic about its use. It is interesting to see that the Egyptians, who recognized no standard alphabetic order for the sounds of their language, categorized their signs by type – animals, plants, human figures, parts of buildings. This is the method of listing hieroglyphs adopted by Sir Alan Gardiner in his Egyptian Grammar, the standard work for all modern students of the ancient Egyptian language. The Egyptian alphabet, so called, is arranged roughly following the Semitic alphabetic system and is only a modern convenience for the compilation of dictionaries and vocabularies.

35. Examples of 'linear' or 'cursive' hieroglyphs, as often used on papyri, with equivalent ordinary signs.

The hieroglyphs used on papyrus were somewhat different from those carved in stone. They were usually drawn in outline with only the barest detail necessary to differentiate signs of a similar shape. Thus the human figures which determine names and the actions of the mouth such as speaking or eating are shown with exaggerated arms since it is by the position of the arms that the two signs may be told apart. The figure used to determine the names of gods and that used to represent a king are even more similar. The distinguishing features are a beard which curls up at the end for the god, and the uraeus serpent at the brow of the king. These signs are called linear or cursive hieroglyphs and were used on the very best examples of the funerary book known as the Book of the Dead. Papyri of this sort were prepared in the 'House of Life', the scriptorium of the temple, where the student scribes were also taught. These scrolls, some of them highly decorative with beautiful vignettes

36. A temple scribe who kept account of offerings made in the king's name or, perhaps, to the king as a living god.

Translation: To the *ka* of the King's Scribe, Scribe of the Offering Tables of the Lord of the Two Lands, the Steward Any, justified

illustrating important chapters, were the Egyptian equivalents of the illuminated manuscripts produced in medieval monasteries by scholar monks. Those students whose handwriting was good enough or who showed an aptitude for designing and painting the necessary pictures could be employed for life in such work.

The title 'Priest of the House of Life' is probably best interpreted as 'scholar' or 'teacher', rather than 'priest'. These priests would be responsible also for writing liturgical books such as those shown being held by the lector priest at a funeral service. Any priest would be expected to have a basic education but to take part in the temple rituals, to read the sacred books and recite the litany of the god, he would need to have undergone specialized training in the 'House of Life'.

There would have been many scribes of lesser rank employed in any temple in positions such as clerk, archivist and recorder (fig.36). The temple estates which supplied all the needs of the god and his servants required large numbers of workers and

37. The accountant Amenemhet, from his Theban tomb. The painted reliefs suffered damage at the hands of Akhenaten's iconoclasts. Each mention of the god Amen has been removed.

Translation (columns read right to left): The Scribe of the Counting of the Grain in the granary of [Amen], Foreman of the Steward to the Vizier, Foreman of the Weavers of [Amen], [Amen]-em-het, justified

administrators. There were many opportunities for scribes within the temple personnel (fig.37).

After the basic training a scribe could specialize in a discipline such as accountancy, law or medicine. There were centres of further education at the larger temples, for instance at the Temple of Horus in Edfu where there seems to have been a medical school. Architects and artists trained as scribes at the same time as learning the skills of their profession in apprenticeship. The artists who prepared the scenes to be painted on the walls of tombs and who drew the outlines for reliefs to be carved in stone did not necessarily complete every stage of the work themselves. They would make the original designs which would then be transferred to the intended site by means of an enlargement grid. Before the colours were applied or the first chisel stroke was made, the scribe-draughtsman would check the outlines drawn by his minions and correct any errors in line or proportion. The title of a draughtsman or painter whose name was Ahmose is given at the head of this chapter. Although the artists' subordinates may have been apprentice-draughtsmen themselves it was not always the case that they understood the inscriptions they were being asked to paint or carve. Checking details of the hieroglyphs was the responsibility of the senior draughtsman, but even then mistakes could be over-looked or appear at too late a stage in the work to be corrected. So many hieroglyphs are similar in their general shape that it was quite possible for a wrong sign to creep into a text, or for signs to be omitted, or for a sign to be inserted in the wrong place.

From the New Kingdom, and probably earlier, some scribes would have specialized in foreign languages so that the king could correspond with fellow monarchs of neighbouring kingdoms. Since Egyptian was the only language to be written in hieroglyphs, most foreign correspondence was conducted in the diplomatic and widely understood language Akkadian, which was written in the cuneiform script. Letters to foreign rulers had to be translated and transcribed, from the original Egyptian versions dictated by the king or his ministers, into an appropriate language. Replies then had to be interpreted and transcribed into Egyptian so that copies could be kept in the archive. Such specialist scribes must have existed though none is known by name and even the rendering of titles thought to mean 'translator' or 'interpreter' are uncertain.

The exhortations to the student indicate that a scribe was exempt from taxation and received many privileges, but the true picture of life as a scribe was probably far removed from this ideal. Much of the work of an ordinary clerk would have been repetitious and tedious. His dues to the state were paid in terms of his work which had to be prolific in order to fulfil the bureaucratic requirements of his masters. Documents often had to be drawn up in triplicate and neither carbon paper nor photocopiers existed in ancient Egypt. It is thanks to their determination to record everything in writing that we know as much as we do about the Egyptian civilization. The depth of our knowledge is largely due to the work of numberless scribes; sadly, for the most part, they are now nameless, though their spirits may live on in their surviving work, as was hoped by the author of a New Kingdom text:

> As to those learned scribes from early days, they who foretold the future, their names have become everlasting even though they themselves have died and all their family are forgotten. They did not make for themselves enduring tombs and stelae, they left no children to remember their names. They made heirs for themselves out of the books which they composed. . . . The writing-board is as a loving son to them, the reed-pen is their child, the stone surface their wife. People of all ranks are as their children for the scribe is their leader. Though their houses have crumbled and their graves are forgotten, as long as their name is spoken through the books which they made when they lived, happy will be the memory of their authors. It is for ever and all time!

Table 11 gives some of the words and titles associated with the profession of scribe.

𓊹𓈖𓏪	The God's Words (hieroglyphs)		script of documents (demotic)		script of Ionia (Greek)
	House of Life (temple school)		House of Scrolls (library)		school
	book, scroll		letter, despatch		pupil
	King's Scribe		secretary, clerk		Scribe of the House of Life (teacher)
	Chief Scribe		Chief Scribe		Hearing Scribe (one who wrote from dictation)
	Scribe of sealed things (confidential)		Scribe of Divine Offerings		Scribe of Sacred Texts
	Overseer of Public Records		Scribe of the Grain Count (accountant)		Registrar of Fields
	Scribe of the Record Office		Wages Clerk		Letter Carrier
	Scribe of Recruits		Army Scribe		Translator, Interpreter

Table 11: Words and Titles Associated with Scribes

6. OFFICIALDOM

The Egyptian state, for most of its 3000-year existence, was a stable society. There were times of unrest, of political and even religious upheaval, but these were of relatively short duration compared with the prosperous and settled periods in between. The major factor in this stability, lying at the heart of the civilization in every respect, was the Nile. The river was the life-blood of Egypt. Without its reliability in providing water for man and beast and for irrigating the fields, people would not have been drawn to settle in the Nile Valley and the civilization would have never arisen. Without the annual inundation which deposited mineral-rich alluvium throughout the length of the valley, the land would not have been fertile enough to support a large, settled population. Without the great highway providing direct communication between centres of population, a unified state would have been an impossibility.

Egypt's wealth was based on agriculture and this required a settled lifestyle. The wealth of a community depended on the amount of land it could claim to provide it not only with food but also with a surplus which could be traded for commodities in which the community was not self-sufficient. The surplus could also be used to support workers and craftsmen who did not make their living directly from the land. Potters, weavers and stonemasons, for example, possessed skills which were necessary to a successful and developing society. As a community grew, both in terms of population and the territory which it commanded, further non-productive personnel were required to organize and administer its resources. Clearly, the man who could lay claim to the largest area of land and who therefore provided the largest single contribution towards the wealth of the community, would have the biggest say in how that wealth should be distributed.

In a democratic society a leader might be elected on the strength of his personality, his business acumen or his honesty. In ancient Egypt a leader, in addition to these atttibutes, had to be a figure of authority, such as a landowner who could call on the loyalty of the peasants who worked his land and who could afford also to support a large number of non-agricultural workers. The size of a leader's following in terms of his family and dependent workers was also a factor in considering the security of the community. A less-than-scrupulous man might be tempted to use this power to impose his will on the community by force and intimidation, whereas a true leader would use his human resources to protect the community from potential enemies such as envious neighbours, itinerant bandits or even foreign invaders. In gratitude for this protection the community would agree to set aside part of its wealth to help support the retinue of its leader. This additional income increased the wealth that was available to the leader for his personal use. He could then afford to commission luxury goods such as fine furniture, jewellery and non-functional monuments.

The development of secular power was paralleled by a claim to spiritual authority. A competent leader would attribute his success to the establishment of an understanding between himself and the local deity. A god favoured those who showed him due reverence and would reward them by bringing prosperity to his chosen people. Ultimately the leader could claim a very special relationship with the god, a kinship which implied the divinity of the leader himself. Thus, at the head of the administration was the divine king, strong, wealthy, devout, perhaps charismatic, certainly authoritarian and the epitome of success.

One of the earliest documents found in the Main Deposit at Hierakonpolis was a commemorative mace-head dating from the period immediately before the 'Unification', (fig.38). The principal figure in the relief on this pear-shaped limestone relic is a king, identified as such by the royal regalia that he wears including the 'White Crown' and the animal tail hanging from his belt. In front of his face there are two hieroglyphs; the symbol of a scorpion which is surmounted by a rosette or eight-petalled flower. This may be his name or a title, it is not clear which, but this ruler is commonly

38. Part of the relief from the Scorpion King Mace-head. The King's name appears in primitive hieroglyphs in front of his face. Behind him stand two fan-bearers and to the far left, other courtiers including one seated in a litter. Above are standards representing districts or towns.

known as the 'Scorpion King'. Around the top of the mace-head is a frieze formed by standards, each bearing the totem or fetish of a tribe or locality. From each standard-pole a lapwing is suspended by its neck. The lapwing hieroglyph represents 'people', so each standard represents a captive or subject people of the 'Scorpion King'. The frieze is not merely decorative, it is a statement of the king's authority.

The king is not alone in this scene. He is surrounded by people, some of whom may have been priests or bodyguards and one, who may have been the king's consort, is shown seated in a litter. Closest to the king stand two fan-bearers. The fan was a semi-circular arrangement of ostrich plumes mounted on a tall pole. It was used to shade the king from the sun rather than to waft a cool breeze over him. Fan-bearers appear in many royal scenes from all periods of Egyptian history, and the title 'Fan-bearer on the Right of the King' was one of great prestige. Sometimes, as in the reign of Ramesses II, royal princes were accorded this honour but the position of 'Fan-Bearer' was not always held by a member of the king's family. As a symbol of this high court rank a man carried a single ostrich feather mounted on a short wand which was used as the hieroglyph for the title itself (see fig.26, page 66).

Another courtier accompanying the 'Scorpion King' is his sandal-bearer who also carries a jar of water with which he would wash his master's feet. Any servant who was allowed to touch the royal person, as the sandal-bearer was bound to do, was in a highly privileged position. King Narmer's sandal-bearer is shown in the extract from the Narmer Palette at the head of this chapter. Personal attendants of this type had to be trustworthy and loyal beyond question. They could, by nature of their close association with the king, exert considerable influence upon him. In much later times concern was expressed about the way in which the king was surrounded by self-seeking courtiers, often personal servants who used their position of trust to pull strings and affect government decisions. The conspiracy to assassinate Ramesses III largely comprised just such servants, several with the title which is usually translated as 'Butler' but which had far wider political and influential significance at the time than is conveyed by the modern word (see fig.51, page 140).

Among the people portrayed surrounding the 'Scorpion King' must be his closest followers including family, friends and advisors: Proximity to the king was a great honour which was not always dependent on kinship with the royal house. The most intimate companions of the king, those who were as near to being personal friends of the monarch as anyone could be in ancient Egypt, proudly proclaimed themselves to be 'known to the King', *nesu rekh*, which is usually translated as 'King's Acquaintance'. Certain 'Royal Acquaintances' also held administrative or religious posts but the term 'known to the King' took pride of place over all other titles. Officials often claimed to be the 'one true follower of the King', which may be abbreviated to 'Sole Companion'. There were so many 'Sole Companions' of the king at any one time that this title seems to have had less substance than the claim to be a 'King's Acquaintance'. A title which might best be translated as 'Privy Counsellor' was that of 'Master of the Secrets of the Palace'. The duties of a 'Royal Acquaintance' or a 'Privy Counsellor' are not at all well defined.

39. Part of a false-door stela from the Old Kingdom. The tomb-owner, on the left, has his titles repeated in the central panel. His wife and son face him from the right.

Translation (man, reading right to left): Sole Companion, Controller of the Palace, with authority over *Nekheb*, [el-Kab], Setj-wabu
(Centre, reading right to left): Sole Companion, Controller of the Palace, Master of the Secrets [Privy Councillor] of the House of the Morning, Official of the House of Life, Setj-wabu (woman, reading left to right): King's Acquaintance, Priestess of Hathor, Priestess of Neith, Nub-hotep (child); His son, of his body, Setj-wabu

In certain religious texts, notably the *Amduat*, literally the *Book of What is in the Other World*, the sun-god Re is described as being served by 'crews' of other deities. The word used is the same as that used for the crew of a boat or a gang of workmen (fig.40). These deities constitute Re's courtiers and are shown in illustrated versions of the text, like that painted on the walls of the tomb of Thutmose III in the Valley of Kings, manning the solar bark on which the supreme god traverses the waterways of the underworld. Teams of deities may also be shown towing the bark and in some cases they are portrayed as jackals harnessed to the prow of the boat like huskies to a sled. The symbol of a standing jackal was used to mean

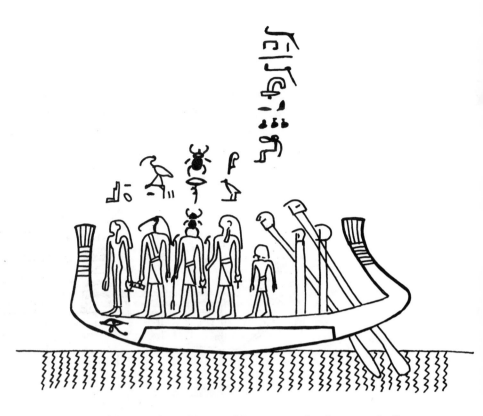

40. A boat of the Underworld crewed by a party of gods. From the funerary papyrus of Nu, in the British Museum.

Translation (above each figure, reading left to right): Isis; Thoth; Khepri; Shu; the Chancellor's Steward, Nu.

Courtier, or Dignitary, a title which would appear to imply a somewhat lesser rank than that of *nesu rekh* or even 'Sole Companion'. The same could be said of the title expressed by the sign of a standing goat with an ornamental collar from which hangs a cylinder seal. The seal was used almost as a badge of office for administrators and there were many 'Seal-Bearers of the King', especially in the Old Kingdom, whose precise duties are undefined. The goat sign may be used to mean 'dignitary' or 'worthy' and indicates a social rank more than a specific administrative post.

There are other titles which do not relate to any particular duty or area of authority. These are similar to European noble titles like Lord or Earl. The Egyptian title *repa* is usually translated as 'Hereditary Prince' and although it is sometimes applied to a member of the royal family, it more often designates a member of the Egyptian aristocracy, a western equivalent being, perhaps, a Duke. In the Third Dynasty the most important of the courtiers in the following of King Djoser was the architect of the Step Pyramid, Imhotep. He held many titles and was canonized in later times to become the demi-god and patron of doctors and scientists. He was *repa* and 'King's Seal-Bearer' as well as being 'Ruler of the Palace' (fig.41).

41. Relief from the reign of King Djoser, giving the name and titles of the architect of the Step Pyramid. To the far right is the *djed* pillar, symbol of stability and emblem of Osiris.

Translation (reading right to left): Seal-bearer of the King, Ruler of the Mansion, Hereditary Prince, greatly beloved, Imhotep . . .

The great land-owning families in their provincial centres could make or break a government. In times of political uncertainty or natural disaster such as famine, people turned to their local rulers, the most powerful of these being the nomarchs or provincial governors. One such man was Ankhtifi, the Nomarch of the Hierakonpolitan province who described his acqisition by conquest of the neighbouring province of Edfu:

> Horus brought me to the nome of Edfu for life, prosperity, health, to reestablish it, which I did for Horus wished it so.

I found the province inundated like a marsh, abandoned by those who had lived there, in the grip of rebels, under the control of a traitor. I made a man embrace his father's murderer and the murderer of his brother, so as to reestablish the nome of Edfu. What a glorious day it was on which peace was restored to this nome. No burning contentious power will be tolerated now that the forces of evil, which the people hate, have been suppressed.

It was with the support of such men of power that Amenemhet I became the first ruler of the Twelfth Dynasty following a military coup, but it is thought that they also were responsible for his downfall. The document called *The Instruction of King Amenemhet I for his Son Senusert I* purports to be a warning from beyond the grave:

Beware of subjects who are not known to you, of their plotting you cannot be aware. Trust neither brother nor friend, make no close acquaintances, it is all worthless. Keep yourself to yourself for no man can claim the loyalty of his followers when the evil day comes. I was generous to the beggar, I cared for the orphan, I gave to the poor as to the rich; but he who ate my food raised opposition against me, he whom I trusted plotted against me.

In the Middle Kingdom, the nomarchs were like the Barons of medieval England who imposed the Magna Carta upon King John. When the government fragmented after the Twelfth Dynasty authority devolved to the provinces and local princes who held titles like *repa* or *haty-aa* became autonomous rulers in their own regions. Occasionally one such prince or family of princes would emerge as a supreme authority over enough territory to be able to claim kingship. At times two or more such 'kings' ruled simultaneously from different centres.

From about 1650 BC the northern part of Egypt was ruled from the Delta which had been taken over by foreign immigrants, whom the Egyptians called simply 'rulers of foreign lands', *Heqau Khasut*. This name has become, in common usage, the Hyksos, and the fact that the Egyptians also referred to these people as *Aamu* or Asiatics indicates that originally they probably came from the region of

[119

Palestine and Syria. The term *heqa* may be used to designate the king himself but is also used for high-ranking officials in which case it is translated as Governor (*see fig. 41*).

The Egyptians themselves were never comfortable admitting the sovereignty of foreigners and were not prepared to accord these 'princes' full regal titles. The local princely family of Thebes was the focus for a rebellion against the Hyksos that led to the hated foreigners being expelled from the country. The Thebans succeeded in reuniting the Two Lands under their kingship without having to rely upon the support of other provincial nobles. They did not repeat the mistake of their Middle Kingdom ancestors but kept a tight rein on the powers of the landed aristocracy. The title *haty-aa*, which had been that accorded to a nomarch, became far less prestigious under the Eighteenth Dynasty. Many more officials bore the title which can be equated to Count or even Sir. As time went on the title was devalued even further so that it came to denote the mayor of a town or a local headman.

Although the significance of titles varied from age to age, one constant in the organization of government was the Vizier. This is an oriental-sounding title commonly used to describe the Egyptian Tjaty but it hardly does justice to the real importance of the ancient office. The figure standing immediately in front of King Narmer on the great commemorative palette represents a highly favoured or influential courtier, as seen in the drawing at the head of this chapter. His name, or more probably his title, is written with the rope tether sign which has the alphabetic value 'tj' as in the word Tjaty. This could be the earliest documented instance of the office which was without doubt the most important and arduous of all government appointments. The title was usually written with the symbol of a duckling or pigeon squab, its stubby winglets outspread and its beak agape, tongue out, squawking. The fact that this hieroglyph is obviously used as a phonetic sign gives no indication as to the origin or derivation of the title Tjaty. It is also used in the word for 'male' and this may indicate that the Vizier was seen as 'The Man' just as the king was called 'The God'. The Tjaty was the 'First Subject' of the king and as such claimed the greatest authority of any mortal.

Although the office of Tjaty was of very ancient origin, the nature of the Vizier's duties changed over the centuries. During the Old Kingdom it was common to find a member of the royal family, perhaps even a 'King's Son' acting as Vizier. Towards the end of the period, in the Fifth and Sixth Dynasties, Viziers were of noble but non-royal families which were sometimes linked to royalty by marriage. The Tjaty Mereruka who served King Teti of the early Sixth Dynasty, was married to the king's daughter whose name was Har-watet-khet (see fig.14, page 40). The family of the nomarch of the province around Abydos included the Vizier Djau who served the last three kings of the Sixth Dynasty. He was brother-in-law twice over to Pepi I and thus maternal uncle to both Merenre and Pepi II. Since his youngest nephew was no more than six years old when he became king, Vizier Djau and his sister the dowager Queen Ankh-es-en-Meryre II acted as regents and advisors to the young monarch.

During the Middle Kingdom the office of Vizier seems to have been shared for much of the time between two Tjatys, one representing Lower and the other Upper Egyptian interests. This division of labour may have been a deliberate attempt to restrict the power of any one man. The last king of the Eleventh Dynasty is thought to have been the victim of a coup instigated by his Vizier, Amenemhet, who became king in his place as Amenemhet I. Having taken advantage of his position as Tjaty in this way it is highly probable that he would have taken every precaution to avoid suffering the same fate as his predecessor. It seems he failed as we saw from The Instruction of King Amenemhet. The Thirteenth Dynasty was, in part, a succession of kings who came from a single family of Viziers, but their authority was restricted by the presence in Egypt by that time of the Hyksos rulers, (fig.42).

As part of the overall curb set on the authority of the Egyptian noble families, the New Kingdom monarchs appointed to the position of Vizier able administrators, men who may well have come from families who had served the Crown in a similar capacity for several generations but who knew that they owed their position only to the king's goodwill. A form of job description or contract of employment was accepted by the holders of the Vizierate and

42. The Vizier Useramen, whose name was often shortened to User, patron of the Scribe Amenemhet who served as the Vizier's Steward, among other positions, during the reign of Thutmose III. From Amenemhet's Theban tomb.

Translation (columns read left to right): The Hereditary Prince greatly beloved courtier, he whose words cause satisfaction in the entire land, Overseer of the Double Treasury of Silver and Gold, Overseer of the Town, Tjaty, User, justified; his beloved wife, Lady of the House, Tjuiu, justified.

several of them had the important text inscribed in their tombs. Most notable of these is the tomb of Rekhmire who was installed as Tjaty in the reign of Thutmose III. There are two distinct texts, the first being the *Installation of the Vizier* in which the ceremony of the Tjaty's appointment is described and he is reminded of the responsibilities as well as the rewards of the office: 'Then His Majesty spoke to him, saying, "Attend to the office of Vizier, be meticulous over everything done in the name of that office, for it is the support of the whole land. Indeed, the viziership is not sweet, it is truly as bitter as gall." '

The second text is a less literary work which is more in the form of a list of all aspects of the Vizier's authority. It is now called *The Duties of the Vizier* and is thought to have its origins in the later part of the Middle Kingdom. This text was designed to remind the Tjaty of and instruct him in the traditions, protocol and administrative procedures of his office. It describes in great detail the range of functions he was expected to perform as First Minister of State and especially as head of the judiciary. The Vizier's court was the ultimate appeal court in civil cases – particularly those involving property rights – although criminal cases were most often dealt with locally and in a summary manner. He had authority over the royal messenger service and was responsible for the upkeep of the national archive. He could call to account tax assessors from their regions and could hire and fire any civil servant of whatever rank. He received foreign tribute in the King's name and controlled the exploitation of natural resources such as stone quarries and timber. Unlike a modern Prime Minister or President the *Tjaty* took little part in foreign affairs. That was left to the king and the army.

In the pyramid-shaped structure of the ancient Egyptian administration, at least during the New Kingdom, there were three major government departments. The Treasurer was nominally of lesser rank than the *Tjaty* in that he had to report to the Vizier each day but he also had the right to be told of all decisions which affected his department and the daily consultation was a two-way sharing of information. Since there was no coinage in use in Egypt, the basis of the country's wealth was grain and the storehouses or granaries in which the annual tithe was collected were the equivalents of bank vaults. So too were the storehouses in which were kept valuable goods such as the produce of foreign tributary territories. The title which is now understood as Treasurer was *Imy-r Per Hedj*, which is literally 'Overseer of the House of Silver'. Another very powerful Treasury official was the 'Overseer of the Double Granary' who would be the principal banker. The holder of the title 'Overseer of Cattle' was not, as might be thought, a minister for agriculture. Cattle were highly valued and, as can be seen in the Cairo Museum's model of the cattle census from the Eleventh-Dynasty tomb of Meketre, and the painting of a similar scene from the Eighteenth-Dynasty tomb of Nebamun, now displayed in the British Museum, livestock represented wealth. Only a rich man could afford to maintain a large herd of cattle and beef was a rich man's meat, although lesser mortals might aspire to have beef requested in their funerary and mortuary offerings. The livestock census was held every two years and records of this were sent to the relevant Treasury official who would issue a demand for a proportion of the herd as payment of taxes. The 'Overseer of Cattle' was, like the 'Overseer of Granaries', a finance minister (fig.43).

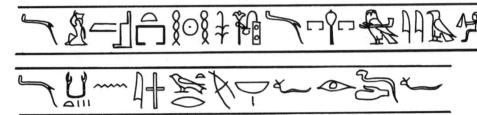

43. Some of the titles of Maya, a prominent court official at the end of the Eighteenth Dynasty, from the wooden model of a funerary bier which he presented to the funeral of Tutankhamen.

Translation (reads left to right):
1. Overseer of Works in the Place of Eternity, King's Scribe, Overseer of the Treasury, Maya, the venerated
2. Overseer of Works in the Great Place, beloved of his master, doing according to his words . . .

During the reign of Horemheb the king employed, as his Chief Finance Minister, a man called Maya. According to his own biographical inscription in his Memphite tomb, Maya had been brought up at court with the prince who was to become king as Akhenaten. He served under Tutankhamen as 'Overseer of Works' on the West Bank at Thebes which means that he was responsible for the excavation of the king's tomb and the building of his mortuary temple. He was also, in all probability, the official who organized Tutankhamen's funeral and the preparation and collection of the tomb goods. His dedicatory gift to his master's funeral was a model funerary bed on which are inscribed his names and titles. Although Horemheb tried to deny the existence of Tutankhamen he could not ignore the talent of Maya whom he put in charge of the wealth of the whole country.

The designation imy-r is one of the most widely used of all official titles and the translation 'overseer' hardly conveys the importance of the rank or the variety of uses to which it was put. The sign used

44. Four scarab seal impressions giving names and titles of private individuals.

Translation: Top left: Great Overseer of the Office of the Treasury, Nem-sekhet-uf
Top right: The Army Scribe, Nehy, born of the Lady of the House, Kisen, justified
Lower left: Overseer of the Cattle of Amen, Sen-neferu
Lower right: Dignitary of the King's House, Royal Seal-Bearer, Overseer of the Seal, Hor

for the abbreviated form of the title is the tongue of an ox which is thought to represent the punning idea of 'being in the mouth'. This could mean a person who speaks with the authority of someone else, who is the mouthpiece of his master. Many important titles include the imy-r element and in either of its two forms it is one of the most easily recognized of all Egyptian titles (fig.44).

The personal wealth of the king in the form of land, possessions and revenues was administered by the composite department of the Royal Domain. The chief ministers in this area of government were the Chancellor and the Chief Steward, both of which titles include the element imy-r. The Chancellor was 'Overseer of the Seal', a reference to the seal worn as a badge of his office. Seals impressed in clay, mud or wax were used to mark ownership and to secure documents, doors and containers. Presumably the seal referred to in the Chancellor's title was the royal seal or one very similar to it. The Chancellor was responsible for the king's revenues and was therefore in a position which could easily be abused. Towards the end of the Nineteenth Dynasty the Chancellor Bay used his position to commission a tomb for himself in the Valley of Kings. That a commoner should have been so blatant in his aspirations to grandeur demonstrates a confidence that must have stemmed from a very close understanding with the Crown. It is thought that Bay acted as advisor to the widowed Queen Tausert and her son or stepson Siptah and that, when the king died at a relatively young age, the Chancellor encouraged Tausert to take the throne in her own right. It is also strongly suspected that Bay was not a native-born Egyptian but came of Asiatic stock. This is not really surprising for at the time there were large numbers of foreigners working in Egypt and anyone who displayed talent in whatever field of expertise could hope to obtain advancement, though few reached the same heights as Bay.

The Chief Steward was more concerned with the day-to-day housekeeping of the royal estates and residences. This is reflected in his title which may be translated as 'Overseer of the Great House'. There were other stewards, each appointed as majordomo of one of the king's residences or those of the senior members of the royal family. Some travelled with the king in his progresses around the country, for the court stayed in several different places in the course of a year. Other stewards and household personnel were based at one particular royal residence such as the summer palace at Abu Gurob on the edge of the Fayum.

Each of the principal officers of state had numerous lesser officials under his command. There were inspectors, guardians and overseers of every description, some specializing in one particular area of administration, others with a wider and less well-defined remit. Some titles which, to modern understanding, seem to be trivial or meaningless have probably lost much of their significance in translation. It is no longer possible to differentiate among ranks within the Egyptian civil service and, since the whole society was hierarchical, there must have been differences which are no longer apparent. A man who called himself *repa* or *haty-aa* often added to this prestigious designation a string of what appear to be minor official titles (fig.45).

The title *adj-mer* which, literally translated, means 'digger of canals' is usually rendered as 'Administrator'. It does not imply that the holder of this title was a navvy but that, originally, the post was associated with the organization of irrigation works and the exploitation of the inundation.

45. Some of the titles of Amenemhet known as Surer, who served Amenhotep III. His mother appears to have been a woman of the royal harem. From his tomb at Thebes.

Translation: Hereditary Prince (*repa*), Nomarch (*haty-aa*), Sole Companion who is active on [behalf of] his Lord, Overseer of Horn, Hoof and Feather (?), King's Scribe, his beloved, Amen-em-het, say of him Surer, venerated, born of the Royal Ornament Mut-tui, justified

The Department of the Army only came into being during the New Kingdom. Until the Theban princes began the expansion of Egypt's traditional frontiers by force of arms there had been no need for a standing army. When danger threatened, usually in the form of foreign invasion or border disputes, a defensive army was levied from the provinces and was disbanded again as soon as the emergency was past. Only a small contingent of royal bodyguards was maintained on a permanent basis. The warrior kings of the Eighteenth, Nineteenth and Twentieth Dynasties brought about a great change in the nature of Egyptian warfare and sought to exert their influence over ever wider areas of the Middle East. There they came into conflict with the other major civilizations of the region, especially the Hittites, the Babylonians and the Assyrians, and the disputed territories of Palestine and Syria were constantly changing hands. The army was nominally under the control of the king himself. Horemheb was the first king to publish details of the formal organization of the Egyptian army and to arrange for permanent troops to be stationed at both extremes of the country so that response to a threat, whether from the north or the south could be as swift as possible. There was an army bureaucracy of staff officers, logistics and supply officials and clerks. Horemheb himself started his career as a 'Scribe of Army Recruits' (see fig.44).

The royal princes were often senior army officers. Several of the sons of Ramesses II are shown in reliefs at Karnak, the Ramesseum and Abydos taking a very active part in the king's military campaigns just as their father had done in the reign of his father, Seti I. Prince Amenhirkhopshef, son of Ramesses III, whose tomb is one of the gems of the Valley of Queens, bore the title 'Overseer of the King's Horse'. This title is sometimes translated as Cavalry Commander but this is misleading since the Egyptian horse troops were not strictly cavalry but chariotry. At the head of the military was the 'Great Overseer of the Army', the Commander-in-Chief. Several career officers held court rank as well as titles such as 'Overseer of the Troops', which is best described as General, and 'Overseer of the Fleet', which might be given as Admiral. There was no navy as such since the Egyptians rarely went to sea but there were transport ships available on the Nile to take troops wherever they were required and these were captained by professional sailors who were counted as army personnel.

As part of the spoils of war, the Egyptian army brought back vast numbers of foreign captives who were disposed throughout the Two Lands as labourers on national projects such as the building of temples, maintenance of irrigation works and in the mines and quarries. Slavery, as understood in modern or even Greek and Roman terms, was non-existent in Egypt. Prisoners of war became integrated into Egyptian society, often intermarrying with the native population although there was a tendency to retain ethnic names

46. Hieroglyphic grafitto from the Island of Seheil near Aswan. The text commemorates a visit by the 'Overseer of Works' responsible for the cutting of obelisks for Queen Hatshepsut in the nearby granite quarries.

Translation (read right to left): King's Acquaintance, his (sic) true beloved, Controller of the Work on the two great obelisks, High Priest of Khnum, Satis and Anukis, Amen-hotep

and customs. Generations of Egyptians with foreign antecedents grew up to consider Egypt their homeland. Some rose to high office as indicated by the proliferation of foreign names, particularly Libyan names, at the court of Ramesses III.

Responsibility for the labour gangs, whether of peasant Egyptians or foreign prisoners of war, was in the hands of the equivalent of a Public Works Department. The 'Chief Overseer of Works' was often an architect by training but also had to be an expert in man-management. He had all the resources of the royal corvée at his command and access to vast quantities of materials such as stone, wood and metals. (fig.46).

One important department which only came into being at the very start of the Eighteenth Dynasty is that of the 'Governor of the Southern Lands', the southern lands being Nubia. The territories of Kush and Wawat were traditionally tributary to Egypt's king and parades of Nubian tribute-bearers bringing the produce of their lands are shown in many tomb scenes like that of Sobekhotep, now in the British Museum. To administer the collection and delivery of tribute and to keep the Nubians under the Egyptian yoke, a permanent military presence was maintained in several purpose-built fortresses south of the First Cataract. A subsidiary capital was established at Faras where the Governor had his official residence. He was also known as the 'King's Son of Kush' which has given rise to the use of the title Viceroy for this official. The Viceroy of Kush was not necessarily a royal prince though it is possible that in the earliest instances the appointees were from a collateral branch of the king's family. The title 'King's Son' was used to convey authority. Faras and the second administrative centre of Soleb were very far away from the Egyptian court. Communications took many weeks if not months and decisions had to be made on the spot.

The Governor of the South was accorded honorary royal status in order for him to act in the king's name on his own initiative without consultation. The appointment was a very great honour despite the fact that it necessitated long periods of absence from Egypt if not almost permanent exile. The Governor had his own court and governmental structure which mimicked in almost every way those of the Two Lands. A new Viceroy was installed in his office during the reign of Tutankhamen. He was Amenhotep known as Huy and the ceremonies and celebrations attendant on his investiture are shown on the walls of his tomb at Thebes.

As in any society, the system of bureaucracy in Egypt was open to abuse. There is a well-documented dispute between the two mayors of Eastern and Western Thebes, each in turn accusing the other of involvement in tomb robbery and fraudulent conversion of stolen property. A passage in the Great Harris Papyrus which details the donations made to the temples during the reign of Ramesses III seems to indicate the suppression of a rebellion instigated by a Vizier in the Delta town of Athribis. However the Egyptian bureaucrat strove not only to obtain favour in the sight of his masters so that he would appear with a clear conscience to make his confession before the 'Judges of the Dead', but also to conduct his life in the way of Maet, the right and proper way for a man to live. This idealism is reflected in the *Instruction of Ptah-hotep*, a rather pompous book of etiquette and guidance which purports to be the work of the Vizier Ptah-hotep who served the Sixth-Dynasty King Isesi. This text was used as copy material by student scribes in the hope that its exhortations to generosity, truth and justice in all things and to all people would be taken to heart:

> If you are a leader of men, who controls the affairs of others, seek to do good wherever possible so that your conduct may be seen to be blameless. Great and lasting in its effects is justice, unchallenged since the time of Osiris himself. . . . If you are a leader of men, with far-reaching authority, you should do outstanding things. . . . If you are a leader of men, listen patiently to the speech of one who pleads. Do not stop him saying what he has to say. When a man is in distress he needs to pour out his heart to someone who will hear whether or not it will win his case. Not every plea can be granted but a good hearing soothes the heart.

Table 12 gives the hieroglyphic terms, in abbreviated form where applicable, for the titles and offices which are most commonly found on personal monuments such as tomb stelae and portrait-statues. The heading for the table is the word for 'ranks' or 'offices'.

	Tjaty (Vizier)		dignitary
	Overseer of the City		official, dignitary
	Hereditary Prince		Master of the Secrets
	King's Acquaintance		local prince, nomarch, mayor, headman
	Sole Companion		elder, chief
	fan-bearer		chief
	official, noble		provincial administrator (lit. Digger of Canals)
	Courtier, noble		district official
	follower, attendant		ruler
	King's Seal-Bearer		inspector
	Chancellor		controller
	Treasurer		keeper, guardian
	Overseer of the Granary		deputy
or	Overseer		judge
	Steward		official, magistrate
	Overseer of Works		revered, worthy (used of deceased)

Table 12: Officialdom

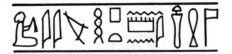

7. THE PRIESTHOOD

Next to the civil service, the greatest opportunity for employment was in the personnel of the many temples throughout the country. Above all else, a temple was seen as the home of the god and his family and, like any other home of quality, it required servants to attend to the owner's needs. The expression most often translated as 'priest' was hem-netjer, meaning 'servant of the god'. Sometimes it may be rendered as 'prophet' though there is little evidence to show that the Egyptian priesthood dealt much in prophesy or mysticism. The simple, descriptive title 'God's Servant' says all.

Priests in ancient Egypt were not concerned with the ethical, moral or spiritual welfare of the people: they had no duty to instruct a flock of worshippers in the appropriate religious rituals nor to interpret sacred texts; and there was no congregation to be led in prayer or to listen to sermons. A priest's duty was primarily to see to the comfort of his god who was the ruler of his mansion, just as much as the king was the lord of his palace. As the king had many servants at his command so too did the gods, and if the king was the greatest individual landowner in Egypt, so the gods owned property which was in every way comparable with the royal domain.

The principal official at a temple was known as the 'First Servant of the God' which is usually translated as High Priest. Just such an influential position was held by Mery-Ptah, High Priest of Amen at Karnak during the early Nineteenth Dynasty. His name and title appear at the head of this chapter. The position of High Priest of a cult was often held by a senior court official. Amenhotep, the architect and 'Overseer of Works' in the reign of Hatshepsut, was also 'First Prophet' of the Aswan triad Khnum, Satis and Anukis.

Since in the course of conducting his office he must have visited the granite quarries at Aswan on a fairly regular basis, it made sense for him to pay suitable respect to the gods of that region. In his absence there were undoubtedly deputy priests who would see to the daily ritual (see fig.46, page 128).

Certain High Priests had secondary titles which were specific to the god they served. The High Priest of Re at Heliopolis was called 'Greatest of Seers' or 'Great of Sight'. The First Prophet of Ptah at Memphis was known as the 'Greatest of Craftsmen' or the 'Master Artificer', a title almost analagous to the 'Master Craftsman' of Masonic tradition.

The High Priest of Amen-Re at Karnak achieved a unique position during the New Kingdom when the Amen temple foundation formed a separate department within the national administration. The role of Amen's First Prophet was a highly political one and was often held by a courtier of superior rank, or possibly a member of the royal family. The power of this sacerdotal official was considerable both in terms of the wealth and the manpower he could command. He was also in a strong position to influence political decisions since the kings regularly sought the god's approval for their actions.

In the reign of Hatshepsut it was said that during a progress in his sacred bark about the Karnak Temple the god Amen had stopped at a point called, significantly, the 'Station of the King', and had refused to move until he had recognized a young acolyte by bowing to the lad. The boy was the Queen's stepson who had been crowned co-regent with her but who had then been pushed into the background when Hatshepsut took the throne as sole monarch. The young king, Thutmose III, used this story to illustrate his legitimacy both as the son of his father and the protégé of Amen-Re. The bowing of the sacred bark must have been condoned if not arranged by the High Priest of Amen. It was a necessary action to counter Hatshepsut's own claim to be the divine child of the god himself.

The 'Servants of the God' were ranked as the senior servitors at the temple. These included the 'Second Prophet' who was effectively deputy High Priest. Such posts were generally hereditary and required as much administrative expertise as religious devotion

47. Part of an inscription from a lintel in the tomb of a Sixth Dynasty priest who served at the pyramid temple of Pepi II.

Translation: Wab-Priest of the Pyramid of (Nefer-ka-Re), the Established and Beautiful, Der-sendj

since the temple was a business. Priests were, in theory, appointed by the king. As part of his 'Restoration Decree', Tutankhamen declared that he had re-established the priesthood, appointing clergy from good families to serve at all the major shrines. Certain permanent members of the temple staff, the career priests, may have started their service as the lowliest of all priests, the *webau* or 'Purified Ones'. Over a period of years they could rise through the hierarchy to become 'Fathers of the God', the next rank below the 'Prophets'.

The majority of priests at any temple served on a part-time basis with priestly duties being organized on a shift system. The priest-hood was divided into four phyles, each serving for one month in four during the year. This meant that any lay priest would work at the temple for three months of the year in one-month periods. In between these periods of service, he could marry and raise a family, conduct business and continue with his usual job or profession (fig.47).

A man would usually serve at a temple dedicated to the god most closely associated with his trade. Thus architects and scribes became priests of Thoth, builders and craftsmen served Ptah and doctors might well enter a temple of Sakhmet. The Tjaty, as head of the judiciary, was High Priest of Maet, the goddess revered by all judges, lawyers and magistrates though she had no major cult centre of her own.

While acting as a 'Purified One', a priest had to observe the rule of purification implied by his title. He would have to shave all the hair from his body, cut his nails, wear only pure white linen and abstain from sexual relations. Priests also had to be circumcised though this seems to have been a generally accepted social custom throughout the population and not specific to priests. There were also taboos on certain foods, notably fish, and the wearing of clothing made from wool. The holy offices could only be con-ducted after ritual lustration with water from the sacred lake of the

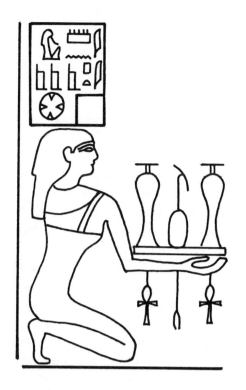

48. The Temple of Karnak personified, from the red-granite chapel built by Hatshepsut, now displayed in the Open Air Museum. The 'mansion' symbol on the head of the offering-bearer contains the temple's name *Ipet-eswt*.

temple, cleansing of the mouth, breath and body with natron, and fumigation with incense. All this was necessary before a priest could come before the god.

The king was *de facto* the premier priest of all cults but delegated his role to his appointees. The reliefs and painted scenes on the temple walls illustrated the rituals conducted within the various halls and chapels and in all of them the king is shown in the role of High Priest. It would have been impossible for him to have performed every ritual in every temple in the land, but the portrayal of him, with the appropriate inscriptions describing the rituals, was a statement of intent. The god would know that the High Priest was carrying out those same rituals as the king's proxy.

The daily ritual mirrored the life of the king himself. The temple was laid out along the same lines as a palace. There was an open, colonnaded courtyard inside the main gate beyond which there were columned halls which represented the formal reception rooms of a noble mansion. Beyond these state apartments were the private quarters of the god and his family which were known by the term *ipet*, the word used for the personal rooms and especially the harem quarters of the royal palace, essentially the home of the god. The Karnak Temple itself was known as Ipet Eswt, the 'Home of Thrones' (fig.48).

The Temple of Luxor, seen as a more personal residence for Amen and his consort Mut, was called Ipet Reswt, the 'Southern Harem'. The greatest of the festivals celebrated at Thebes was simply known as the 'Feast of Ipet', when Amen and Mut spent their annual holiday at their second home. At the centre of the ipet was the sanctuary which represented the god's bedroom. This was usually surrounded by suites of rooms including the lesser shrines for the god's spouse and child and any other subsidiary deities recognized at the temple. There were also spare rooms for visiting deities and storerooms for all the god's personal possessions. The walls of these rooms were decorated according to their use so that illustrations of the sacred barks and the rituals performed before them show which chapel was dedicated to which deity. Reliefs also show the types of object kept in each storeroom. There were large numbers of ritual vessels, vases, lamps, offering stands and libation jars. The god's wardrobe and his jewellery were also kept near at hand and the precious oils, unguents and incense used in the rituals were stored close to the heart of the temple for safety.

The innermost recess of the sanctuary was the shrine which held the cult statue of the god. This statue which was thought to hold the spirit of the god himself could have been made of wood, or carved from stone, or cast or beaten from precious metal. In front of the stone shrine in which the portable wooden shrine stood, was a stone block on which the bark of the god could be rested. This may easily be mistaken for an altar but, in fact, Egyptian religious rites did not include the use of a sacrificial table. The food offerings made to the god were placed on stone offering-slabs which imitated simple reed mats, or the type of offering-stand with a central pillar support, which could be easily moved as required in the course of the ritual.

At dawn the god was awakened by the singing of a morning hymn. The doors of the shrine were opened and the god's statue removed. Music and chanted prayers accompanied the ablution and purification of the statue, the clothing and the application of cosmetics, and then the first meal of the day was presented to the god. Libations of water were poured over the food set out for the god's delectation. Incense was burned in bowls and saucers, and flowers decorated the offering-tables. All the god's senses were thus indulged. When the offerings had rested before him long enough for the god to have taken his fill, they were removed to the lesser offering-tables of the temple where his family and companions could also partake of the meal. Once they too had been satisfied, the offerings were removed back to the temple commissaries from where they would be distributed to the temple employees. This was the way in which the priests and all the subsidiary temple workers were paid for their labours. One of the advantages of serving a tour of priestly duty was the quality and quantity of the wages. Two further meals were served to the god, at midday and in the evening, and after the third the cult statue was returned to its shrine for the night and the doors were sealed (fig.49).

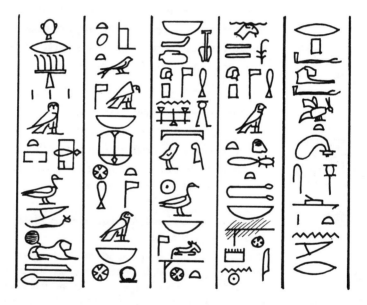

49. Part of a late Twenty-fifth Dynasty inscription, on a lintel in the Cairo Museum, originally from a tomb in the area of Heliopolis. The full text gives details of thirteen generations of a priestly family from that region.

Translation (columns read right to left): Count and prince, Royal Seal-bearer, beloved Sole Companion, High Priest of Heryshef-nesu-tawy, High Priest of Horus Khenty-khety, Lord of Athribis, Chief Prophet of Amen-Re, Lord of Sem-behdet, Chief Prophet of Onuris-Shu, Son of Re, Lord of Sebennytos, Prophet of the Great Isis, Mother of the God, Lady of Hebyt, Prophet of Horus. Lord of Shen, Controller of Offering Tables in the Great Temple, *sa-mer-ef* [a priestly rank associated with the cult of Heryshef], Kher, justified

The preparation of the offerings, the maintenance of the temple and the care of the god's possessions required a veritable army of craftsmen and domestic staff who were not necessarily priests. The estates which provided all the raw materials for the offerings employed farmers, fishermen, herdsmen and wildfowlers. Communication between the estates in different parts of the country was conducted by means of the god's fleet of boats with their crews who could also be called upon for escort duty when the god himself went on progress or visited another temple. Builders, masons, sculptors, painters and smiths were all needed to maintain the fabric of the temple. Spinners, weavers, needlewomen and launderers saw to the production and care of the god's clothing, the priests' vestments and any other textiles such as curtains which shielded the shrine from the impure gaze of ordinary mortals when the god was out and about in his bark. Ramesses III recorded the appointments he made to the Temple of Re at Heliopolis (fig.50):

> I appointed for thee archers and collectors of honey, bearers
> of incense to deliver their yearly tithe into thine august treasury.
> I appointed for thee hunting archers to capture white oryx . . .
> I made for thee boatmen and tax-officials. . . I appointed servants
> as watchmen of thy harbour . . . I made door-keepers . . . and
> guardians of the grain stores.

50. Part of the inscription in rudimentary hieroglyphs from a Twenty-seventh Dynasty kneeling statue.

Translation (columns read right to left): Made by his son, who does what he wishes, the Priest of Bastet, Ny-ka-Sebek, known as Hor; born of the Lady of the House, Sistrum Player of Khuit, she who clothes the god, Bastet-em-heb . . . Any *wab*-priest who will enter into or depart from the temple, who will protect [my] statue for [me] when he says my name . . . the like shall be done for him in the presence of the Great God, Lord of Athribis . . .

Meat offerings were prepared in the temple abattoir by specialist slaughtermen. The joints were inspected by priests and had to be declared pure before being offered to the god. There was no blood sacrifice on altars before the god. Blood was considered impure. Kitchens staffed by many cooks provided the wide variety of baked goods which were thought necessary for the god's satisfaction. The words for 'satisfy' and 'offering' were written with the same sign, an offering-mat bearing a single loaf of bread. In the lists of offerings made by Ramesses III the many types of loaf are numbered in hundreds of thousands.

The bigger the temple, the larger the staff it required and the greater the estates needed to support it. The satellite buildings around the outside of the temple proper but within the mudbrick temenos wall, included workshops, kitchens and animal pens as well as the living quarters of the priests. There would also be the administrative offices where the scribes worked, keeping records of all the temple's business such as the day-to-day deliveries of produce from the god's estates. Each temple had its own treasurer, granary overseer and taxation officer. The god levied taxes on his tenants, the farmers who worked his land and the artisans who lived in his villages. Temples were also repositories for official documents such as wills and details of property transactions and archivists kept records of the events of the king's reign. One such priestly scribe named Manetho, from the city of Sebennytos, was commissioned by his Ptolemaic masters to write a history of Egypt in Greek. It is due to Manetho's work, which must have been compiled from the records of earlier scribes, that modern Egyptologists divide up the ancient history of the country into dynasties.

Temples were the seats of learning, the universities of ancient Egypt. Most of the religious literature, such as the *Hymns of Praise*, must have originated in the temples, written by scribes of the sacred texts. Standard versions of such prayers or liturgy were written down to be recited by lector-priests who would read them without deviation from the proper text. The priest who enacted the ritual recited by the lector was known as the Sem or Setem Priest. As celebrant he was identified by the leopard- or cheetah-skin garment worn over his shoulders. This may have been an imitation animal-skin like that included in Tutankhamen's tomb. This was made of woven fabric studded with bronze sequins representing spots and had a carved and gilded cheetah's head attached to it (see fig.4, page 20).

The music and chanting which accompanied such liturgy were performed by specially trained musicians and singers. Harpists,

51. Musicians from the Theban tomb of Amenemhet.

Translation (left to right):
1. The Favoured One [female singer], Baket
2. [words of the lutanist's song] A beautiful day, for spending a happy time
3. Amen-em-het
4. Ruiu-resti
5. The butler, Tjeny

flautists and percussionists were all employed as temple musicians but the sacred-ritual instrument was the sistrum, a rattle with a hooped head across which were held jingles similar to those on a tambourine. The hollow head of the rattle was often shaped like the head of Hathor with whom the instrument was most closely associated. The title 'Sistrum Player' could also mean 'Priest of Hathor'. Singers and dancers entertained the god, especially at festival times when professional acrobats and jugglers were also employed (fig.51).

Even in the older periods there were some female priests, usually associated with the cults of goddesses such as Hathor, Isis and Bastet, but on the whole the priesthood was male (see fig.14, page 40, and fig.39, page 116). The musicians, however, could be male or female and the position of Chantress was a very respectable profession for a woman. The female personnel at a temple were called, collectively, the 'Favoured Ones' which is the same term used to mean concubines. This should not be interpreted as meaning nuns or priestesses like the Vestal Virgins of Rome. The 'Favoured Ones', like lay priests, could marry and have families.

It is not clear to what degree the purification rituals of the *webau* applied to female temple staff as women did not have such close contact with the god as male priests. The woman in overall charge of the 'Favoured Ones' bore the title 'Matron of the God's Harem'. Tjuya, the mother of Queen Tiye and grandmother of Akhenaten, bore such a title in the cult of the fertility god Min at Akhmin.

At the beginning of the Eighteenth Dynasty the title 'God's Wife' was often held by the Queen. This was a religious rather than a purely royal title and was passed from mother to daughter or sister to sister for several generations. This was a different and perhaps antecedent appellation from that of 'God's Wife of Amen' which became very important from the Twenty-first Dynasty. The kings of this period ruled from their Delta capital of Tanis while the religious heart of the country, Thebes, came increasingly under the autonomous control of the 'High Priests of Amen'. One such High Priest, Herihor, had himself represented in reliefs at Karnak officiating at rituals in the role traditionally reserved for the king. Herihor gradually assumed all the titles and regalia of royalty and claimed the titles Commander-in-Chief and Ruler. His successors continued to have supremacy over the Thebaid while remaining on good terms with the Tanite kings and successive northern princesses moved south to become the wives of the High Priests. The authority of the High Priests extended far into the southern lands so that they were able to call themselves Viceroys of Nubia and even Viziers. Their royal consorts adopted the title 'God's Wife of Amen' and, as such, held many sacerdotal titles. The 'God's Wife of Amen' Neskhonsu, wife of Pinedjem II, claimed the following titles in inscriptions on her coffin:

> First Chief of the Favoured Ones of Amen-Re, King of the Gods; Matron of the House of Mut the Great, Lady of Ashru; Prophetess of Anhur-Shu, the Son of Re; Prophetess of Min, Horus and Isis in Akhmin; Prophetess of Horus, Lord of Djuef; God's Mother of Khonsu the Child; First One of Amen-Re, King of the Gods; Chief of Noble Ladies.

Pinedjem II was the grandson of the first High Priest to have officially claimed the kingship. The area covered by his wife's priestly titles shows that the influence of the priest-kings of Thebes stretched well into Middle Egypt.

With the emphasis on the religious nature of the kingship, the rulers of Thebes often appealed to Amen-Re for advice on political matters. Oracular decisions indicated by the bowing or halting of the god's bark were sought on several well-documented occasions including once when the hereditary rights of the Princess Maet-ka-Re were decided by the Theban triad, Amen, Mut and Khonsu. By the latter part of the Twenty-first Dynasty the title 'God's Wife of Amen' was held by a royal daughter who was then consecrated to the god as his wife. She became the 'Divine Adoratrice', the 'Hand of the God', a celibate priestess who continued to wield considerable political influence. She officiated at the temple in rites previously performed by the king or the High Priest. Her name was written in cartouche as befitted a representative of royal power who was also accepted by the priesthood. When Thebes finally lost its independence to a new dynasty of kings from Nubia, the incumbent 'God's Wife of Amen', the daughter of the last king of the Twenty-third Dynasty, was forced to adopt the daughter of the new king as her successor, indicating the political importance placed on the role of 'High Priestess of Amen' by the Nubians. The chapels which were built as mortuary-shrines for the 'God's Wives of Amen' of the Twenty-fifth Dynasty are still to be seen at Medinet Habu. The sarcophagus of the 'God's Wife of Amen' Ankhes-en-nefer-ib-Re, the last holder of the title, is on display in the British Museum.

Apart from the temples of the gods there were other places of employment for priests, notably the mortuary cults of the kings. In the Old Kingdom these temples were attached to the royal pyramid-tombs around which small townships arose to house and provide offices for the temple personnel. (see fig.47, page 134). By the New Kingdom the kings had separated the building of tomb and mortuary temple so that the shrines to the memory of the deceased monarchs were built on the valley floor beneath the western cliffs at Thebes. Each mortuary temple was endowed by its builder with lands to provide revenues for the maintenance of those offerings which would ensure his immortality. Some of these mortuary temples were also dedicated to national deities for whom daily rituals were conducted while the kings in whose honours the temples were built were still alive.

A royal mortuary temple was usually called the 'Mansion of Millions of Years', expressing the king's wish for eternal life. Unfortunately the mortuary foundations were not as long-lasting as their owners intended they should be. The largest royal mortuary building ever to be built at Thebes was the temple of Amenhotep III. The opulence of this monument was described on a massive stela erected within it. There were gold- and bronze-plated doors, columns inlaid with gold, silver and semi-precious stones, and pavements of shining white alabaster. This 'Mansion of Millions of Years' was razed to the ground within 150 years of its foundation, its stone used to build the mortuary temple of King Merenptah. Even the stela was reused. It was carved with the record of Merenptah's military victories and is commonly called the Israel Stela. All that remains of the temple are the two guardian-statues which stood before the entrance pylon. These are now known as the Colossi of Memnon. The Mansion known as Medinet Habu, built as the mortuary temple of Ramesses III in the Twentieth Dynasty, became the centre for the administration of the whole of the royal necropolis. The offices of the local Vizier and taxation officials were there as were the storehouses in which were kept the king's valuables, probably including the goods intended for his tomb.

The tombs of those ordinary Egyptians who could afford to provide tombs for themselves included small chapels or offering-areas which served the same purpose, albeit on a more modest scale, as the royal mortuary temples. Usually the celebrant at the funeral service and at subsequent mortuary rituals would be the heir of the deceased. If the family was wealthy enough, professional priests would be employed to undertake these duties, their fees being provided from the revenues of a funerary endowment. There were numerous priests employed at each major necropolis, some attached to royal mortuary temples or the shrines of funerary deities such as Osiris and Sokar. Others were the 'ka-priests' who attended to the mortuary chapels of private tombs.

The rituals observed in such chapels varied from the simple recitation of the offering formula as recorded on the funerary stela, to the full mortuary service which involved offerings of food, drink, flowers, incense and prayers. The chapels were also used regularly by the families of the deceased who would gather there for acts of remembrance. Such gatherings were the nearest equivalent in ancient Egypt to communal worship during which the living and the dead shared a family meal and the younger generations discussed their problems and sought answers from their worthy ancestors. The chapels would be cleaned and repainted and the graveshaft opened as necessary for further interments. Some chapels in the Workmen's Village at Amarna were provided with small garden plots and cooking areas indicating that they were used or at least visited frequently. This was religion on a very personal basis.

Though the gods, through their temples, employed enormous numbers of people in all capacities, not all of those employees by any means were priests, and of those with sacerdotal titles the majority were only part-time priests. For most every-day religious requirements the ordinary Egyptian people could quite easily dispense with priestly services altogether if they were prepared to do it themselves. However out of respect and honour for their deities it was only right that they should continue to offer their services as servants in the houses of the gods. Bringing themselves to the attention of the gods by making themselves useful could only be beneficial when they came before the ultimate deity, Osiris, at the entrance to Eternity.

At the head of Table 13 is the hieroglyphic term for a phyle of priests. The table includes titles associated with temple personnel, not all of them priests, and some words for the buildings and places in which they worked.

𓊪𓊪	prophet, priest (lit. servant of the god)	𓊪𓊪𓊪	First Prophet, High Priest
𓊪𓊪 or 𓊪	Father of the God	𓊪𓊪	Purified One, ordinary priest
𓅓𓅓	Sem (Setem), celebrant priest	𓅓𓅓	Chief Priest
𓏏𓏏𓏏	Lector Priest	𓏏𓏏𓏏	The Priesthood
𓏏𓏏 or 𓏏𓏏	Priest in charge of offering tables	𓏏𓏏	divine offerings
𓏏𓏏𓏏	musicians, singers (*masc*)	𓏏𓏏𓏏	musicians, singers (*fem*)
𓏏𓏏𓏏	sistrum player (priest of Hathor)	𓏏𓏏	chantress
𓏏𓏏𓏏	(*masc*) dancers (*fem*)	𓏏𓏏𓏏	
𓏏𓏏𓏏	star watcher, astronomer, keeper of calendar	𓏏𓏏𓏏	Favoured Ones (female temple personnel)
𓏏 , 𓏏	ka priest, (of mortuary cult)	𓏏𓏏𓏏	temple
𓏏 , 𓏏 , 𓏏		𓏏 , 𓏏 , 𓏏	shrine, chapel
𓏏𓏏 , 𓏏𓏏	necropolis	𓏏𓏏 , 𓏏	sanctuary

Table 13: The Priesthood

8. THE SERVANTS IN THE PLACE OF TRUTH

Very few working-class Egyptians could afford a proper Osirian burial. The best they could hope for was to be remembered by their own relatives or, if they were employed by a wealthy family, to have their portraits included in the tombs of their masters. Seneb and Kahap, two of the stewards in the household of the Fifth-Dynasty Vizier Ptah-hotep, had their names and titles recorded in the reliefs in their lord's tomb. In the same tomb the 'Inspector of Scribes' Seshem-nefer is even mentioned by his nickname, Tjefu. In the Saqqara tomb of Mereruka, tucked away in a corner of a detailed relief showing life along the river, is a small boat bearing the designer himself, the equivalent of the artist's signature. Even these examples are of middle-class citizens who may have had modest tombs of their own in the less fashionable parts of the Saqqara necropolis. The ordinary Egyptian peasants shown in such scenes are, for the most part, anonymous.

There is evidence that some townspeople usurped older tombs in order to provide a burial place for themselves and their families. Collections of coffins from several different periods have been found in many tombs. In some cases extra shafts or chambers were roughly cut to accommodate such subsidiary burials after the original tomb had been entered by robbers. The names of the usurping tomb-occupants were inscribed on their coffins and mummy bandages and probably on what few pieces of burial furniture they were afforded, but since often these secondary burials were subsequently ransacked in their turn, most of the deceased have lost their identities. In the Twenty-first Dynasty several intrusive burials were made in the tombs of the two preceding dynasties at Memphis. On

the remains of one such coffin found in the tomb of Iurudef, what appears initially to be a hieroglyphic inscription on closer examination is found to be gibberish. A few genuine hieroglyphs had been included to lend an air of authenticity but clearly the 'scribe' who drew them was hardly more literate than his customer (fig.52).

52. Meaningless coffin inscription from the cache of subsidiary burials in the Memphite tomb of Iurudef.

Very few areas of ancient settlement are now available for excavation in Egypt since most are still sites of occupation. The few ancient towns or villages that have been investigated cannot be considered as typical examples of ancient Egyptian settlements. These include the Middle Kingdom town of the pyramid-builders at Kahun and the village of the workmen who serviced the city of Akhetaten, neither of which had developed from an ancient settlement. They were built for a very specific purpose and their inhabitants were draughted in according to their skills or the services they provided. Both were occupied for a fairly short period, hardly a generation in the case of Amarna.

The community which left the greatest archaeological legacy was the village which is now known as Deir el-Medina, hidden in the Theban hills a mile away from the Valley of Kings. In ancient times this was called the 'Place of Truth' and its people were among the most privileged of their class in all Egypt, and certainly the most literate, as is shown by the wealth of documentary evidence from the village. Most of the villagers were craftsmen chosen for the quality of their work for they were commissioned to excavate, build and decorate the tombs in the two 'Royal Valleys'. The 'Valley of Kings' was known to them as the 'Great Place' and, by tradition, Amenhotep I was the first king to have his tomb built in this area, separate from his mortuary temple. He and his mother, Ahmose-Nefertari, were considered to be the patrons of the village so that by the beginning of the Nineteenth Dynasty, they were worshipped as the local deities of the community with their own shrines and festival days (fig.53).

The chapel of Amenhotep I was the most prominent among those which stood in the open area outside the northern gate of the village. During the time of the festival of the deified king and his mother, their statues were paraded around the village and even taken as far as the 'Great Place' to inspect and bless the work in progress. The workmen donated many statues of themselves to Amenhotep I, often seeking his advice or help in a wide variety of personal matters, such as the interpretation of dreams, the finding of lost or stolen property and the likelihood of promotion at work. The royal patrons were also portrayed on the funerary stelae of the Workmen as in that belonging to the Foreman Neferhotep.

The men who built the earliest tombs of the Eighteenth Dynasty seem to have been established in the village only for as long as it took to build each sepulchre. They were charged with completing the work as quickly and secretly as possible, hence the choice of the village site which was a convenient distance from the Valley of Kings from which the workmen could come and go unobserved. The supervision of the workmen was originally among the duties of the 'Overseer of Royal Works'.

In the reign of Thutmose I, when the first tomb was excavated in the Valley proper, the official in charge of the work was Ineni who also had responsibility for the king's building projects at Karnak. Sometimes, as in the case of Hatshepsut, the 'High Priest of Amen' took on the role of supervisor of the tomb. In the reign of

53. Stela of the Foreman Neferhotep showing the owner paying homage to the deified Amenhotep I and the king's mother, Queen Ahmose-Nefertari.

Translation: (the king): The Good God, Lord of the Two Lands, (Deser-ka-Re), Lord of Appearances, (Amen-hotep)
(the queen): (Ah-mes Nefertari) who lives
(above the man): Son of the Foreman of the Gang, Neb-nefer, justified Nefer-(em)-hotep
(columns right to left): Words made as offerings to the Good God. . . . Son of Re, Lord of Appearances (Amen-hotep), given life . . . and to his mother, the Great Wife of the King (Ah-mes Nefertari), who lives, that they might give Life, Prosperity and Health to the *ka* of the Foreman of the Gang in the Place of Truth, Nefer-hotep, justified

Tutankhamen the Treasury official Maya doubled as 'Overseer of Works' on the West Bank (see fig.43, page 124). By this time, apart from a hiatus during the reign of Akhenaten, the village had been occupied almost continuously for nearly 150 years since the time of its foundation in about 1500 BC. By the reign of Horemheb at the end of the Eighteenth Dynasty the community appears to have acquired official recognition as land was allocated to village families. It is clear that the position of 'Royal Workman' had become hereditary and there was a permanent population sustained and maintained by the state.

The Vizier was in overall charge of the 'Place of Truth' from the Nineteenth Dynasty. There was a 'Council of Village Elders' who pronounced judgments in disputes of a purely parochial nature but greater matters of discipline and serious crimes such as tomb robbery or sacrilege were referred to the Vizier in Thebes.

The workforce was known as the 'Gang in the Place of Truth', the word 'gang' being the same as that applied to the crew of a ship. The 'Royal Workmen' were known as the 'Servants in the Place of Truth', as shown in the heading of this chapter, the hieroglyph for servant being the ear of an ox which represented the verb 'to hear' or 'to obey'. The number of men employed directly as workmen varied from about thirty at times when no major projects were under way, to about fifty as in the busy period in the middle years of the reign of Ramesses II. In most cases new recruits to the 'Gang' were found from among the sons of existing workmen. One of the senior villagers was appointed 'Overseer of the Youths of the Place of Truth', or 'Apprentice Master'. He would direct the boys and young men of the community and make recommendations as to their promotion to the 'Gang'. The 'Apprentice Master' was usually one of the scribes assigned to the village (fig.54).

The senior scribe of the village held the title 'Scribe of the Tomb'. He was appointed directly by the Vizier and would usually have one or more assistants. By the reign of Ramesses III there were two 'Scribes of the Tomb', working together with several lesser scribes, each assigned to one 'side' of the 'Gang'. The workforce had always been divided into two 'sides' the 'Gang of the Right' and the 'Gang of the Left', designations which originated in the practice of sharing

54. Vignette from the funerary papyrus of a Scribe of the Tomb at Deir el-Medina.

Translation: The Osiris, the Purified, the Scribe in the Place of Truth, Overseer of the Youths of the Horizon of Eternity (Apprentice Master) Neb-hepet, justified

the work between two groups of workmen, each responsible for working on one side of the tomb. It is not clear whether both groups worked in the tomb together or in shifts, nor how rigidly the workmen kept to their allotted 'side' in terms of the work carried out. The Scribe's main job was to keep a day-to-day record of the progress of the work and of the attendance of the workforce. Extracts from the Day Book of the 'Scribe of the Tomb' make illuminating reading. There are details of injuries and accidents suffered, absence for all sorts of reasons from attending a funeral to drunkenness, and the distribution of tools and materials. The 'Scribe of the Tomb' was the intermediary who transmitted the Vizier's orders to the workforce and the Workmen's complaints to the Vizier. He also acted as notary for the village and many personal documents such as wills, contracts of hire or bills of sale were drawn up by 'Scribes of the Tomb' acting in this capacity.

The Scribe was in a position of considerable influence, especially in judicial cases or matters concerning promotion. Many were not above accepting bribes, as is clearly indicated in some surviving documents. Kenhirkhopshef who came to office during the reign of

Ramesses II and served for more than forty years as 'Scribe of the Tomb', was twice accused of bribery and of using undue influence to have 'Royal Workmen' carry out work on his private tomb during official working hours. The position of 'Scribe of the Tomb' was not necessarily hereditary since it called for specialist skills and a degree of education which was not attainable by all. Kenhirkhopshef, who was the son of Pa-nakht, was adopted by the Scribe Ramose as his successor and the younger scribe called both men 'Father'. This is a good example of the use of a term of family relationship which should not be read at face value (fig.55).

55. The Scribe of the Tomb Butehamen from his tomb at Deir el-Medina. The hieroglyphs, which were probably drawn by the Scribe's own hand, are rather poor considering the position he held.

Translation: The Osiris, Scribe in the Place of Truth, Buteh-Amen, justified

The appointment of 'Chief Workman' or 'Foreman of the Gang', either of the 'Right' or the 'Left', was made by the Vizier, ostensibly acting on behalf of the king himself. Nevertheless the position was almost always passed from father to son or from brother to brother. The Foremen and the Scribes were the representatives of the village to whom all correspondence was addressed and who conducted all official business with the authorities in Thebes. The Foremen were responsible for all aspects of supervision of the workforce such as the issue of tools and building materials to the Workmen. When the workload was so demanding that extra labourers had to be conscripted in to the village, the Foremen saw to the allocation of jobs, and when times were not so good, it was the duty of the

Foremen and the Scribes together to decide on redundancies. The titles 'Great One of the Gang' or 'Chief of the Gang' were both used to designate the post now rendered as Foreman as in the tombs of Anherkhau, one of the most attractively decorated tombs in the Theban area. He also called himself 'Overseer of the Work in the Horizon of Eternity'. The royal tomb was called the 'Horizon' because the deceased king was thought to enter the underworld by means of the western horizon as the sun set.

Each Foreman had a Deputy or Assistant who was often a relative, possibly his son, to whom the 'Chief Workman' would delegate some of his duties. The Deputies also acted as Village Councillors and took part in the regular inspection tours around the tombs under construction. They were held responsible for order in the community but their position apparently did not earn them any significant increase in wages. They were listed with the other workmen in the daily rosters and they were lower in the order of precedence than the draughtsman who drew and painted the wonderful coloured reliefs in the tombs of the Nineteenth and Twentieth Dynasties (see the heading to chapter 5, page 96).

Other workmen included carpenters, sculptors and stonemasons who were all specialist craftsmen. With such a wealth of artistic talent available it is not surprising that the tombs of the villagers themselves should be so impressive, rivalling in both colour and detail the tombs of the nobles. It is possible that in slack times some of the 'Servants in the Place of Truth' moonlighted on private tombs such as those on the Asasif above Deir el-Bahri and in the Dra Abu Naga above the Ramesseum, but generally they were kept fully occupied with their royal commissions and helping out each other in their spare time in the preparation of personal sepulchres (fig.56).

The workmen were paid by the state. There was no agricultural land around the village itself though some families owned and worked fields down on the river plain. All the food supplies had to be brought in by donkey train and water must have been delivered daily for there was no natural spring or well at the village. There were many subsidiary workers attached to the 'Place of Truth' who took no direct part in the building of the Tomb. These were the

56. Painting from a *shabti* box from Deir el-Medina.

Translation (reading right to left): The Osiris, the Sculptor in the Place of Truth, Nakht-Amen, justified; his wife, Lady of the House, Nub-em-shaset, justified

porters, water-carriers, woodcutters and caravan masters as well as the wildfowlers, fishermen and gardeners who were employed by the state to provide the food for the village. The wages of the workmen, were paid in kind. The largest part of any man's pay was paid in grain, some of which was used for making bread or brewing beer, the rest being used as currency to barter for other goods. Records of deliveries of foodstuffs show that the villagers were particularly well provided for and on festival occasions they ate very well indeed. The Door-keepers of the Tomb, one for each 'side', took delivery of the provisions and were responsible for their distribution. They were considered to be the bodyguards of the Scribes and were often employed as messengers and as bailiffs who seized the property of debtors and tax-defaulters. As a result a Door-keeper was not the most popular of men within the community.

57. Part of a stela from Deir el-Medina.

Translation: Guardian in the Place of Truth, Nebwy, justified

The security of the Tomb and the Village was principally in the hands of the door-keepers and the 'Guardians'. The 'Guardians of the Tomb' took delivery of building materials and other necessary goods such as the linen used to make wicks for the workmen's candle-lamps. The most precious items in the charge of the 'Guardians' were the tools made of copper and bronze. These had to be weighed before issue and checked again on their return to the store. No tool was ever casually discarded since metal was valuable. Damaged or blunted tools were sent down to the workshops in Thebes for recasting or sharpening, and it was the job of the 'Guardians' to keep track of every tool down to the smallest chisel blade. There are several documented cases of the loss of official tools and the subsequent recriminations and accusations of theft and bribery. The 'Guardians' were also responsible for directing the labours of other village workers such as the mixers of gypsum plaster, the potters and the water-carriers.

Part of a Workman's wages could be paid in terms of hours worked by servants or slaves attached to the village. Each family was allocated a certain number of days of labour according to the status of the head of the household. One record shows that a village matron owned ten days of servant labour per month. She could call upon the village slaves to do menial and time-consuming tasks such as grinding grain, brewing beer, laundering and cleaning, but she could also exchange any or all of these days for other services or goods. The slaves provided for the village by the state were not attached to any one household but their labour was shared on a well-defined basis.

Inspections of the 'Great Place' were carried out at intervals not only to see that the work was progressing well on the current tomb, but also to check on the security of earlier tombs. There were always accusations of tomb robbery flying around the village though very few cases seem to have been proved. A Workman would have to have been desperate to risk his life and family by committing such a heinous crime so close to home. There were officials based in Thebes who might best be described as policemen. These were known as *medjay*, a name deriving ultimately from that of Nubian tribesmen famed for their prowess as archers. In times of war, Medjay troops were draughted into the Egyptian army in whole regiments but in peace-time, acted as law enforcement officers, and the term *medjay* lost its ethnic significance.

The *medjay* associated with the 'Place of Truth' were under the command of the Chief of Police who had his offices at one of the royal mortuary temples. In general the *medjay* were independent of the 'Place of Truth' and received their orders from the Mayor of Western Thebes, but those responsible for the security of the village and the 'Great Place' were closely associated with the Door-keepers and the 'Guardians'. Although the *medjay* were not residents of the 'Place of Truth' they conducted a good deal of business with the villagers. They bought and sold goods and often hired transport in the form of donkeys for their inspection tours.

From the many documents which have survived from Deir el-Medina, it is clear that most of the Workmen, and many of the women too, could read if not also write. Many wills and deeds of transfer of property are known. Several women of the village were independently wealthy as the result of inheritance from parents or husbands. Childless couples adopted children who were not necessarily orphans in order to pass on possessions and position. An example of one such adoption dates from the reign of Ramesses II when the Foreman Neferhotep adopted as his heir the Workman Paneb who was the son of the Workman Nefersenut. This caused a great feud between Paneb and Neferhotep's younger brother Amen-nakht who had hoped to inherit the post of Foreman. When Paneb was made Deputy of the Gang, Amen-nakht objected, considering that he, as Neferhotep's blood-kin, should have been appointed to the position of his brother's assistant rather than the Foreman's adopted son. Various charges were brought against Paneb through the Village Council and even the Vizier's Court, in an attempt to discredit him. When Neferhotep died, it was even suggested that Paneb had mistreated his adoptive father but he still came to be appointed as the old man's successor in the position of Foreman, much to the chagrin of Amen-nakht. Paneb was accused of lascivious conduct, drunkenness, violence and eventually, tomb robbery in which his son, the Deputy Aapahte was also implicated. It seems that Paneb's violent temper and antagonistic attitude towards his adoptive family brought about his downfall. All this may be established from examination of the many documents surviving from the time which covers most of the Nineteenth and early Twentieth Dynasties.

Business for the 'Servants in the Place of Truth' during this period was very good but relations with the administration were often strained. There were constant delays in the delivery of provisions which amounted to late payment of wages. These problems were exacerbated by the distancing of the royal patrons from Thebes as the Ramesside rulers established their capital in the Delta.

Despite complaining letters from the 'Scribe of the Tomb' to the Vizier in Thebes, deliveries of grain were often delayed by more than twenty days and when they did arrive were only a small proportion of what was due. Eventually the Workmen felt so aggrieved that they downed tools and, with the Scribes and the Foremen leading them, marched down to the mortuary temple of Thutmose III where they knew some of their supplies were stored, and carried out a sit-down protest. The following day they did the same at the Ramesseum. They gained the support of the Chief of Police who agreed to negotiate on their behalf. Finally the grain was paid to them but in instalments, some coming from the personal stores of the Vizier, the 'High Priest of Amen' and the Mayor of Thebes. It appears that the storehouses which should have been able to supply all the needs of the village had been sorely depleted as a result of massive embezzlement. Some officials had been lining their own vaults at the expense of the royal stores in the belief that the remote administration would not become aware of the problem. It was inevitably the Workmen at the end of the line of payment who suffered.

Most of the documents from the 'Place of Truth' were written on ostraca in the hieratic script. Some of the handwriting, notably that of Kenhirkhopshef, is very cramped and difficult to read. Hieroglyphs were reserved for the texts on the walls of the Workmen's tombs where it is possible to identify their names and titles and to piece together the rather complicated family relationships. The tombs of Deir el-Medina are small but beautifully decorated and more informative than any of the royal tombs on which the 'Servants in the Place of Truth' laboured.

The titles associated with the 'Royal Workmen' and the other inhabitants of the village are given in Table 14 which is headed with the expression 'The Gang in the Place of Truth'. Such expressions may be identified on funerary stelae and tomb furnishings from Deir el-Medina.

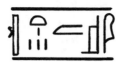

Hieroglyph	Meaning	Hieroglyph	Meaning
	The Place of Truth (Workmen's Village at Deir el-Medina)		The Great Place (The Valley of Kings)
	The Beautiful Place (The Valley of Queens)		The Tomb (royal tomb under construction)
	Servant in the Place of Truth (workman)		workman
	Overseer of the Gang of Workmen		Foreman of the Gang
	Chief Workman		Deputy
	draughtsman, painter		craftsman, carpenter
	sculptor		carpenter, hewer of stone
	stone mason		labourer, porter
	guardian		door-keeper
	messenger		weavers
	workmen		village elders, council, court
	Overseer of the young men (apprentice master)		apprentice

Table 14: The Workmen

9. KEEPING COUNT

The development of a system of writing is often secondary to that of a means of recording numbers. Primitive cave-painters kept tallies, scratched lines or notches carved in bone or wood, presumably to record such things as the number of animals caught in a hunt or the passage of time. These simple strokes, one for each animal or day, are the most basic of all counting methods and predate real writing by thousands of years.

The Egyptian signs for numbers were based on just such a system of one stroke for one unit, but by the pre-dynastic era, further symbols had been introduced to make large figures less cumbersome. These provided signs for the powers of ten: 10, 100, 1000 and so on up to one million. This proves that a base-ten number system was recognized from the very earliest periods of Egyptian society although a place-value notation was never developed. This is different from the Mesopotamian sexagesimal system (base sixty) from which the modern world has inherited the division of hours and angles into powers of sixty. This is one indication of the home-grown nature of the Egyptian civilization.

The Egyptians recorded all manner of information numerically. In fact it is not apparent that they had written words for numbers above two since figures are always used where necessary in even the most decorative of hieroglyphic inscriptions. On the Narmer mace-head the war booty in terms of cattle, goats and living captives is recorded in primitive hieroglyphs, as shown at the head of this chapter, which are clearly the same as the signs used continuously up to the end of the Ptolemaic era. Whether we are to believe Narmer's tally of 1,422,000 goats, 400,000 cattle and 120,000 men is another matter. The number of prisoners of war is quite astounding given that Egypt's population was probably only two million.

In the Medinet Habu reliefs of the campaigns of Ramesses III there are several scenes showing the king reviewing the spoils of war in which the numbers of dead and captured are clearly recorded. The Egyptians counted their slain enemies by removing the right hand and the penis from each body. Scribes are shown making the count of these gruesome relics as they were piled in heaps before them. There seems to have been a bounty paid in the form of a share of the booty, to any soldier who brought in such a trophy. Although the numbers do not tally exactly between the scenes, in the first Libyan campaign it seems that the Egyptians accounted for about 12,000 dead and 1000 prisoners of war. In the reliefs depicting the second clash with the Libyans, the numbers are more precise. A running battle across the eastern desert led to the slaughter of 2175 men and the capture of 2052 people including

58. Princess Nefert-iabet, from a relief in the Louvre. The offerings she requires are listed beneath and around the offering table and are numbered in thousands with the lotus leaf symbol for 1000.

283 youths and 588 females. The Libyans had come with all their families and possessions intending to invade and settle in Egypt. Their domestic animals, taken as war booty, included cattle, sheep and goats, horses and donkeys, to a total of over 42,000 beasts. Compared with these numbers, Narmer's claims appear to be a little on the large side!

In tomb reliefs and on stelae erected in mortuary chapels, numbers were used to indicate the quantities of offerings required by the tomb-owners. These requests were rarely modest, regularly

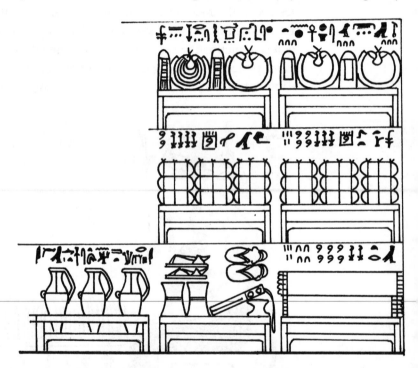

59. Storehouse scene from the Sixth Dynasty tomb of Mehi at Saqqara. Note the sandals and the scribal palette on the 'bottom shelf', centre.

Translation (reading right to left):
Top shelf: (collars) of electrum, 30; of gold, 30; woven of living things, (floral ?) 30; of lapis lazuli; of turquoise; of the Southland (?)
Middle shelf: (. . .) linen, in lengths of 100 cubits, 3405; (. . .) linen, in lengths of 100 cubits, 4200
Bottom shelf: (bundles) of reeds, 2645. . . . wine belonging to the King's Seal-bearer, Sole Companion, Mehi

demanding loaves of bread and jars of beer by the thousand. The
waterlily stem and leaf symbol for 1000 is the most commonly
appearing numeral in such texts. Some offering lists are confined to
basic domestic requirements. The simplest request was for bread
and beer, these being the staples of the Egyptian diet. A wider range
of food items would include ox flesh and wildfowl and perhaps
wine in place of beer. Among the non-food items would be natron
and incense for purification rituals, alabaster and stone wares for
storing the requested oils and salves, and linen for both clothing
and household use. As a blanket statement to cover any necessities
which might have been overlooked, there could also be a request
for 'every living thing', meaning vegetable produce, or 'every sweet
thing', referring to such things as fruit and honey. Sometimes the
quality of the offerings was specified by the statement 'every good
and pure thing on which the gods themselves live' (see fig.68,
page 186).

The more demanding of tomb-owners would have their offerings
drawn up in charts or tables with different types of loaf or cuts of
meat specified and enumerated. Similar tables are to be seen on the
walls of temples where kings recorded their piety in the establishment of offerings to be made to the gods. One such is the table of
offerings of Amenhotep III at Karnak. In the sanctuary of the same
king's temple at Luxor he is shown presenting more, carefully
chosen offerings to Amen, including four oxen each specified by
its colour.

Similar methods were used for recording temple possessions and
the inventories of some of the storerooms which surrounded the
sanctuaries of the temples may still be seen on their walls. These
were permanent records of what each store was expected to contain
under ideal conditions and not necessarily what was held
in store at any particular time. Practical inventories, which were
updated at regular intervals and kept on papyrus or leather rolls
written in hieratic, were more realistic. Inventories of personal
storehouses were often included on the walls of a tomb as a means
of the tomb-owner taking his possessions with him to the next
world. Such pictorial representations of valuables include jars of oil
and wine, bales of cloth, furniture, stonewares and leather goods.

60: Part of the parade of livestock from the estates of the Vizier Ptah-hotap. The different species of bird are identified by features such as the shape of the tail.

Translation (top row, right to left): 121,200; 121,200; 11,110; (bottom row) 120,000; 121,022; 111,200

Vizier Ptah-hotep even had the livestock of his personal estates shown in his tomb at Saqqara. Token examples of the various species of geese and ducks which were to be found in his poultry pens are shown with numerals to indicate the size of their flocks. These numbers may be exaggerated, even for the possessions of the most influential man of the Two Lands (fig.60).

The quantities of goods delivered by way of tithe or taxes to the royal and temple storehouses, and especially to the granaries, were strictly recorded by teams of scribes. In the Deir el-Bahri reliefs of Hatshepsut's trading expedition to the 'Land of Punt', pellets of frankincense resin are shown being measured out by the sackful to be taken back to Egypt for use in temple rituals. The standard sack or basket used for measuring dry goods, especially grain, was the *heqat* which has been calculated to be the equivalent of slightly more than a gallon (4.5 litres). Grain was measured by volume rather than weight so the quality of the grain was not properly taken into consideration. Because grain was used for exchange purposes, smaller quantities than the *heqat* had to be standardized. One tenth part of a *heqat*, was called a hin, designated by a jar of a particular shape. This held the equivalent of about half a litre.

Further smaller divisions of the *heqat* were defined by the so-called 'Horus Eye Fractions', designated by the various parts of the 'Eye of Horus'. This powerful amuletic symbol, also called the 'Healing' or 'Healed Eye', represented the eye lost by Horus during one of his fights with Seth. It was said to have been restored, made perfect, by either Isis, Hathor or Thoth. The 'Horus Eye Fractions' were the reciprocals of the powers of two: a half, a quarter, an eighth and so on down to one sixty-fourth part of a *heqat*. The smallest recognized unit of volume was the *ro*, a mouthful. It was reckoned that five mouthfuls made one sixty-fourth of a *heqat* so there were 320 *ro* to one *heqat*.

Another way of defining the value of an amount of grain was by means of a unit of strength for the beer or bread which could be made from that grain. This 'baking value' or 'cooking ratio' was defined as the number of loaves of a particular type, or jars of beer, which could be made from one *heqat* of grain. The stronger the beer or better quality the bread, the lower the baking value. Beer was measured by the *des* jug which was similar in capacity to the *hin*.

Calculating volumes was obviously a useful skill for accountants who controlled the granaries. The Rhind Mathematical Papyrus in the British Museum includes examples of solutions to problems concerning the capacity of rectangular and cylindrical granaries as well as tables of the 'Horus Eye Fractions' and their equivalents in terms of *hinu*. In order to put these calculations into effect the dimensions of the granaries had to be known.

The standard unit of linear measurement in Egypt was the cubit, defined as the length of the forearm from the point of the elbow to the tip of the middle finger. Since not all people have arms of exactly the same length, the cubit was standardized very early in Egypt's history. The royal cubit, literally 'the cubit of the king', which was used for land measure and building purposes, was approximately 20.6 inches (52.3 cm) which is considerably longer than the Greek or Roman measure of the same name. A short cubit of 17.7 inches (45 cm) was also in use, the difference between the two measurements being one handsbreadth or palm. There were seven palms to a royal cubit and six to a short cubit. Each palm was said to be the width of four fingers or digits, giving 28 digits to a royal cubit. A fingersbreadth in ancient Egyptian terms was the equivalent of 0.75 inches (1.9 cm). The relationship between the cubit and the *heqat* was reckoned to be that 30 *heqats* occupied a volume equal to one cubic cubit.

Cubit measuring-rods marked out in palms, digits and fractions of a digit, may be seen in several museums. Two such, one in the Louvre and the other in Turin, belonged to the Treasury Minister Maya towards the end of the Eighteenth Dynasty. The markings on the Louvre example show that other units of measure were in common use such as the span, which was the distance covered by the spread hand from the tip of the thumb to the tip of the little finger. The digit sections are labelled each with the name of its presiding deity, the first nine being overseen by the gods of the Great Ennead with the exception of Tefenet who is replaced by Horus. Other measuring-rods are known such as those placed with other tools in the tomb of Kha, one of the royal architects during the reign of Amenhotep III.

Precise measurements were necessary for the laying of foundations for buildings. The process of measuring out the plan of a building was called 'stretching the cord' and was thought to be overseen by Seshat, the goddess of writing and record-keeping. The cord mentioned was 100 cubits long with knots at one cubit intervals and is sometimes called a rod. The Fifth-Dynasty Palermo Stone, a document which lists, year by year, the principal events in the reigns of Egypt's earliest kings, includes several references to the 'stretching of the cord' for temples or palaces (see fig.64, page 173).

Among other numerical references on the stone which takes its name from the museum in Sicily in which its largest section is to be seen, are details of shiploads of timber being imported from the Lebanon and the building of new boats from this wood.

The boats were described in two ways, either by their length in cubits or the number of oars required to propel them through the water. Some of the ships mentioned on the Palermo Stone are described as being 100 cubits long which is over 170 feet (52 m). The largest boat so far discovered in Egypt is the solar bark buried beside the Great Pyramid of Khufu at Giza. This vessel is just over 140 feet long (43 m) and, despite five huge oars on either side, may

61. The goddess Seshat, Keeper of Records, from the temple of Senusert I at el-Lisht.

Translation: Foremost of the Temple

have been a barge which had to be towed by other boats. It is not certain that the Khufu ship was ever used on the river. It may have been built specifically to be buried with the king as a *duat-tawy* boat, a boat of the Underworld, as described in the entry on the Palermo Stone for the reign of Khufu's father Seneferu (fig.62).

62. Extract from the Palermo Stone giving details of events during one year in the reign of King Seneferu of the Third Dynasty.

Translation (reading right to left): The building of 35 houses. . . of 122 cattle, the making of a 100 cubit *duat-tawy* boat out of cedarwood, the making of two 100 cubit ships of *meru* wood, the seventh occasion of the numbering, [height of Nile] 5 cubits, 1 palm, 1 digit

Linear measurements were made very accurately considering the primitive methods and tools used by the ancient Egyptians. The huge stone blocks which plugged the ascending corridor of the Great Pyramid are hardly more than half an inch (1.25 cm) narrower and just over an inch (3 cm) lower than the corridor itself. This left very little room for manoeuvre when the blocks were manhandled down the passage from the Grand Gallery above.

Land was surveyed by methods similar to those used by architects to set out the foundation plan of a building. Tax assessors measured fields each year to calculate the area of land under cultivation and to estimate the crop yield. The 'cord' or 'rod' was used for such measurements and the area was calculated as a number of *setat*, or square rods, or in terms of strips of area 100 square cubits, each strip being one cubit wide and 100 cubits in length. In the Ptolemaic era the *setat* became known as an *aroura*. On the basis of the survey a tax demand for about 20 per cent of the expected crop was issued.

In measuring over large areas the Egyptian surveyors were just as accurate as the masons who could cut a stone to a specific size. The base of the Great Pyramid covers an area of slightly more than 13 acres, (just over 5.3 hectares) and yet in shape it is an almost perfect square. The greatest difference in the lengths of the sides is under 8 inches (20 cm) and each corner is within seconds rather than minutes of a true right angle. The sides are aligned with a similar degree of accuracy along north-south and east-west axes. The Rhind Mathematical Papyrus contains examples of calculations to find the angle of slope and the height of just such a pyramid as well as its volume. Another mathematical papyrus in the Moscow Museum of Fine Arts includes a problem on the volume of a truncated pyramid, the sort of calculation that would have been necessary when working out the quantities of stone used in the building of the Great Pyramid. Quarrymen's marks in red ochre on some of the blocks used in the pyramids show that measurements were recorded even by workmen who were otherwise illiterate.

More valuable materials such as metals and semi-precious stones were measured by weight. The unit used for weighing such materials was the *deben*, the equivalent of about 91 grammes or 3.2 ounces. One tenth part of a *deben* was called a *qedet*. Scale weights were made in the shape of rings or different animals for easy identification. The scales used were of the same type as those shown in scenes of the 'Weighing of the Heart', a pair of similar pans suspended from the ends of a centrally balanced beam, similar to the symbol for Libra in the zodiac.

Bronze and copper tools such as chisels, pickaxe heads and knife blades, and household items such as basins, ewers and vases, were valued according to their weight. A broken metal item had a scrap value which was almost the same as that of the undamaged piece. No coinage was used in Egypt until it was introduced under foreign rule. At certain times there were fixed rates of exchange for goods and services based on a barter system. Wages were usually paid in the form of food, chiefly grain, and clothing. A workman or craftsman could purchase goods or pay his taxes by offering his skills and labour in exchange. Exchanges of goods were often effected by allocating notional values to each item in terms of a weight of copper or bronze. This complicated system required the purchaser to gather together goods equalling in their metal value the agreed price for the items he wished to 'buy'. Bills of exchange and contracts of employment show that the system worked.

Foreign rulers considered Egypt to be a rich country. Gold was sent as gifts of friendship between monarchs and one Babylonian ruler demanded more and more gold which, he said, was like dust in the land of his brother, the king of Egypt. Porters bearing tribute from the Asiatic lands of Retjenu (Northern Syria), Palestine and other exotic places such as Crete, are shown bringing vessels of wrought metal – bronze, copper, silver and gold – in foreign designs, while those from the southern, Nubian territories, bring gold in the form of nuggets or dust carried on trays and in bags, or as ingot rings. The weights of metal recorded as being presented to the temples is quite staggering. The Great Harris Papyrus in the British Museum contains an exhaustive record of the royal donations made to temples during the reign of Ramesses III. The following entry comes from the section dealing with the Temple of Re at Heliopolis. Here the weights are given only in *deben* (d) although the original entries are given to a fraction of a *qedet*:

> Fine gold 'of the balances' [in its raw state]   1278d
> Fine gold and electrum in vessels and ornaments   198d
> Silver of the balances and silver in vessels   1891d
> Silver in beaten work   394d
> Black copper [bronze] of the balances   67d
> Copper in beaten work   400d
> Copper in vessels   1416d

The use to which such metals might be put is also described in the papyrus as in this extract from the section dealing with the gifts to the Temple of Ptah at Memphis: 'I made for thee [the god Ptah] statues of the King of gold beaten work: others of pure silver in beaten work likewise, kneeling upon the ground before thee, bearing a vase and an offering table. I made for thee a great vase-stand for thy court, overlaid with fine gold.'

Doors, gateposts and lintels were overlaid with gold or electrum, or with bronze which was itself inlaid with gold. Columns, floors and walls were inlaid with colourful stones such as carnelian, jasper, malachite and turquoise. The quantities of such stones used by Amenhstep III in his building works at the Karnak Temple are listed there on the Third Pylon (fig.63).

63. From a list of the donations made by Amenhotep III to the Karnak Temple. The weights stated are equivalent to approximately 440 kg of turquoise and 620 kg of carnelian.

Translation: Turquoise, to the weight of 4820 deben; carnelian to the weight of 6823 deben

In medical papyri the ingredients of prescriptions are sometimes quantified, especially in the case of valuable substances such as spices or incense. The quantities suggested may be given in ro, a mouthful being the equivalent of a modern tablespoon, or by weight. It seems that very small amounts could be accurately weighed against wheat grains or the seeds of the carob tree, both of which are remarkably uniform in size and weight.

The Egyptians never developed theoretical mathematics but their ability to keep accounts and make practical calculations for purposes such as engineering or surveying was perfectly adequate, if not ingenious. The results in the form of hugely impressive and enduring monuments and a remarkably stable society speak for themselves.

The Egyptian hieroglyphs for numbers and the various units of measurement are to be found in Table 15. At the head of the table is the verb 'to count' or 'to reckon' as used in the expression 'Scribe of the Counting of Grain' which should more realistically be rendered as 'Accountant' (see fig.37, page 108).

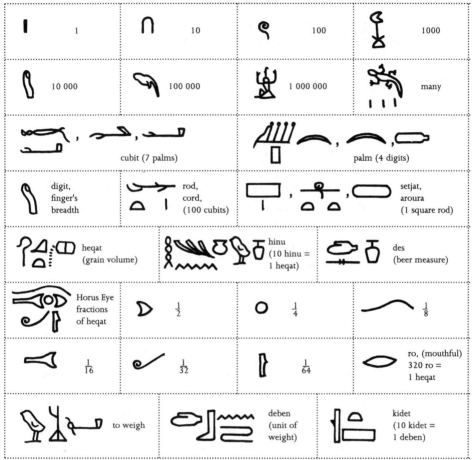

❙ 1	∩ 10	ℂ 100	⚘ 1000
𝄃 10 000	100 000	1 000 000	many
cubit (7 palms)		palm (4 digits)	
digit, finger's breadth	rod, cord, (100 cubits)	setjat, aroura (1 square rod)	
heqat (grain volume)	hinu (10 hinu = 1 heqat)	des (beer measure)	
Horus Eye fractions of heqat	$\frac{1}{2}$	$\frac{1}{4}$	$\frac{1}{8}$
$\frac{1}{16}$	$\frac{1}{32}$	$\frac{1}{64}$	ro, (mouthful) 320 ro = 1 heqat
to weigh	deben (unit of weight)	kidet (10 kidet = 1 deben)	

Table 15: *Keeping Count*

10. MARKING TIME

In recording the passage of time the ancient Egyptians used two calendars which together provided a perfectly adequate system for dating documents and keeping in step with the agricultural cycle on which the country's economy depended. The one event which most directly affected all Egyptians was the inundation. The annual rains in the highlands of what is now Ethiopia caused a rising in the level of the River Nile throughout its length and, as the flood waters were allowed to spread over the fields, the land was enriched with the silt which, by its colour, gave rise to the ancient name, Kem, the 'Black Land'.

It was essential that the people of Egypt knew when the inundation would occur for preparations had to be made well in advance. Dykes and irrigation channels had to be cleared and repaired, cisterns and shadufs readied for use. At several places along the Nile, for instance on the Island of Elephantine at Aswan, measuring devices now known as nilometers were built to keep a record of the levels to which the river rose and fell. The device took the form of a steep stone stairway descending into the water. As the river rose, the water level was closely observed until it had reached its highest point which was marked by carving or painting a record on the wall of the nilometer. The lowest point was also noted so that a value could be set on the 'height' of the inundation. One such record is shown on the Palermo Stone.

The text on the Palermo Stone is divided into rectangular boxes each of which records the events of one year of a king's reign. The boxes are separated from each other by the palm-rib hieroglyph for 'year'. At the bottom of each year-box is a smaller rectangle inside which the height of the inundation for that year is given as a measure in cubits, palms or spans, and digits. By reference to such

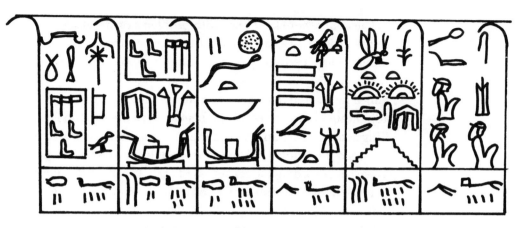

64. Extract from the Palermo Stone dealing with part of the reign of a king who may be Den of the Second Dynasty.

Translation (starting at far right):

1. Smiting the Bedouin (Nile; 4 cubits, 1 span);
2. Appearance of the King of Upper and Lower Egypt; Heb Sed (Nile; 8 cubits, 3 digits)
3. [Numbering of] all the peoples of the north, west, south and east (Nile; 3 cubits, 1 span)
4. Second occasion of the Feast of Djet (Nile; 7 cubits, 2 palms)
5. [design of] the Temple called Thrones of the Gods, Feast of Sokar (Nile; 5 cubits, 2 palms, 2 digits)
6. Stretching the Cord for the Temple called Thrones of the Gods by the priest of Seshat, great door (Nile; 4 cubits, 2 palms)

records kept over centuries, the priests and scribes in charge of the nilometers could calculate whether the flood was good or bad. Disaster and famine lay at both extremes and although nothing could be done about the level of the river, forewarned was forearmed. Contingency arrangements were set in motion in order to alleviate the effects of a bad Nile. In the case of a low Nile these might include handouts of grain from the stockpiles in private stores such as the granaries belonging to the provincial nobles or the local temples. At the other end of the scale village defences had to be protected from possible uncontrolled flooding. In the latter case, boundary-markers and landmarks could be destroyed and as a result there were likely to be disputes over land rights. Every so often it was necessary to survey the land again and to redefine boundaries between properties.

The courts were kept busy with problems of illegal seizure of land or the division of estates in inheritance cases. During the 'Intermediate Periods', when an authoritative central government was non-existent, anarchy prevailed and one of the first tasks of a king if he wanted to be seen as a fair and honest leader, was to adjudicate in such cases. At the beginning of the Twelfth Dynasty King Senusert I set up a boundaries commission whose officers surveyed the whole land and redefined the borders of the provinces as well as recording the resources of each. Details of this Egyptian equivalent of the Domesday Book are to be seen on the kiosk of Senusert I which was originally erected in the Karnak Temple precincts but was later demolished to make way for other buildings. Its stone blocks were used as part of the infill in New Kingdom pylons at the temple and when these were being restored, Senusert's original building was recovered and rebuilt like a three-dimensional jigsaw puzzle. Its clear reliefs were long protected from the elements during its concealment in the New Kingdom pylons. It is now one of the most impressive exhibits in the Open Air Museum at Karnak.

As the inundation was such an important event, its start heralded the beginning of the Egyptian year. This coincided with an astronomical event known as the heliacal rising of Sirius. The Dog Star (Sopdet to the Egyptians, Sothis to the Greeks) and thirty-five other bright stars were called the *Ikhemseku*. They rise heliacally, that is shortly before dawn, at ten-day intervals throughout the year, hence the Greek term which is generally applied to such stars, the decans. After this fleeting appearance at dawn, a decan rises a few minutes earlier each day until, after ten days, another decan becomes the dawn reference-star. Decans were used to gauge the passage of time throughout the night. At the beginning of the ancient Egyptian year, twelve decans rose during the night-time, giving a night of twelve hours' duration in the summer. As Sirius rises heliacally about mid-July by our modern calendar, when day and night are approximately equal in length, the day was also divided into twelve hours. In winter the nights are longer and more decans are seen to rise but the night was still defined as being twelve hours long so the length of an 'hour' in ancient Egypt varied from season to season and from night-time to daytime (fig.65).

65. Part of the 'astronomical' ceiling from the tomb of Seti I in the Valley of Kings. The figures used to mark constellations do not match with modern groupings but the bull, which appears as a haunch of beef in other 'zodiacs', may represent Ursa Major, the Great Bear.

Several tombs include as part of the decoration of their ceilings or walls scenes which are known as 'zodiacs' though there is no evidence for the practice of astrology in Egypt before the Classical period. These take the form of celestial 'maps' with the stars grouped in named constellations for easy recognition. Since the groupings are not the same as those recognized today it is not always possible to identify the ancient constellations with modern equivalents. The ancient zodiacs, like those in the tombs of Seti I and Ramesses VI, concentrate on the stars known to the Egyptians as the 'Imperishable Ones', meaning the stars that never set.

In the tomb of Thutmose III in the Valley of Kings one wall is dedicated to the naming of the stars that presided over the hours of night during which it was thought that the deceased king made the perilous journey with the sun-god to the depths of the Underworld and then rose again to rebirth at dawn on the eastern horizon. Star-watcher priests recorded the rising of the decans and the apparent movements of the 'Imperishable Ones'. The astronomical cycle which governed the agricultural calendar was carefully observed since most religious festivals followed this calendar, especially those associated with the land.

[175

Similarly the phases of the moon were watched. The crescent moon hieroglyph was the abbreviation for the word 'month'. The day of the new moon, called the 'First of the Month', was sacred to Thoth. The 'Festival of the Half-Month' was the day of the full moon. The rulers of the Eighteenth Dynasty seem to have held the moon-god in particular regard since their names were often compounded with that of Thoth, as in Thutmose, or with that of the ancient moon-god, the moon itself, Iah, as in Ahmose. A month in the Egyptian civil calendar at thirty days was slightly longer than a lunar month. The symbol for day was the sun sign, as used for the god Re, which was also the general determinative for all expressions relating to time.

The year was divided into three seasons of four months each, with five extra days known as epagomenal days, an expression of Greek origin. In Egyptian the term used for these days was 'the five days upon the year'. They brought the total to 365 days in a year. The seasons were called 'Inundation', 'Coming Forth' or 'Emergence', and 'Drought'. The last two are often called Winter and Summer respectively. Each day was known by a day, month and season as in the example at the head of this chapter. This is taken from the Rosetta Stone and reads 'second month of Inundation, day 17'. The five extra days were celebrated as the birthdays of Osiris, Horus, Seth, Isis and Nephthys and at different centres throughout the country, New Year's Day was considered sacred to other deities, notably Hathor, and was called the 'Opening of the Year'.

No correction was made for the extra quarter of a day which is needed for a full solar year. This caused the civil calendar to slip apart from the astronomical calendar by just less than one day every four years. During any one person's lifetime this was not evident and for most Egyptians who lived by the agricultural cycle, such a discrepancy was of no real account. This only became a problem for scribes who, at certain times found themselves, for example, dating their work to the season of Inundation when the land was parched dry at the height of summer. Such a situation is described in a papyrus from the Ramesside period: 'Winter has come in summer, the months are reversed, the hours are all in confusion.'

The sliding apart of the calendars righted itself once in every

1450 years, approximately, when the heliacal rising of Sirius again coincided with the beginning of the civil year, the first day of the first month of Inundation, New Year's Day. The Egyptians never saw the need to sort out this muddle but in the Ptolemaic Period Greek minds were bent to the problem, and in 237 BC Ptolemy III proposed the addition of another holiday to set the calendar to right: 'The national festivals kept in winter should come to be kept in summer, the sun changing one day in every four years, and the other feasts now kept in summer should come to be kept in winter in the future as happened in the past.'

The innovation was unsuccessful. The Egyptians continued to used their sliding calendar until they had the Julian calendar imposed upon them by Augustus in 30 BC.

In the course of dynastic history, several scribes mentioned the occasion of the heliacal rising of Sirius but only once, as late as AD 139, was the absolute coincidence of the two calendars recorded. Calculating back in units of 1450 years, or thereabouts, this gives a possible date for the initiation of the civil calendar somewhere between 2780 and 2760 BC. but since it was almost certainly in use before that date, another 1450 years back takes the creation of the Egyptian calendar into the predynastic age. On a papyrus from the temple of el-Lahun at the entrance to the Fayum, the heliacal rising of Sirius is said to have occurred on the twenty-fifth day of the first month of Winter in the seventh year of the reign of Senusert III. This translates to a date around 1872 BC. This is one of the very few 'fixed' dates around which modern Egyptologists have built their chronology.

The records on the Palermo Stone show that a sophisticated system of marking time was already in operation in the earliest years of the dynastic era. This document covers the first five dynasties and was probably a compilation of official records taken from various sources. The division into groups of years assigned to individual kings indicates the usual method of recording the passage of years. There was no single starting point for Egyptian history. Years were numbered according to the length of the monarch's reign so that events, monuments and documents were dated in the form, 'Year X under the Majesty of King N'. When

the king died the numbering system started again for his successor.
This scheme took no account of a co-regency, a period when two
sovereigns, one a younger king crowned during his father's lifetime,
shared the throne. Nor was there any indication of reigns which
may have been concurrent because two or more kings, ruling from
different capitals, claimed sovereignty at the same time. One of the
most important of Egyptian historical records is the Turin Canon,
a hieratic papyrus which lists the kings of Egypt up to the Seven-
teenth Dynasty. This gives a number of years for each king's reign
without indicating any possible gaps or overlaps.

Sometimes, as in the case of partial documents, it is difficult to
decide which year is indicated by a particular reference. On the
Palermo Stone of which three major fragments are to be found in
the museums of Palermo, Cairo and University College, London,
the crucial parts of some reigns which include the names of the
kings themselves, are missing or damaged. It is possible to
reconstruct a sensible timescale by reference to events listed in the

**66. Ivory label of the Second Dynasty, showing King Den smiting an enemy,
representing a military campaign against eastern bedouin tribesmen.**

Translation: (beneath arm of king): Causing the end of . . . [finishing off]
(far right): First occasion of the smiting of the East . . .

existing sections. For instance, the census of livestock which took place every two years is referred to as the 'Occasion of the Numbering'. If a fifth 'Numbering' is mentioned it indicates the ninth or tenth year of the king's reign, depending on whether the first census was held in the first or second year (see fig.62, page 167 and fig.66).

Other such 'dates' are not so useful. On the ivory label from the reign of King Den of the Second Dynasty, the event commemorated is the 'First Occasion of the Smiting of the East', a military campaign against the Bedouin tribes of the eastern desert regions. This is not linked to a numbered year in Den's reign so as an historical hook on which to hang a chronology it is not particularly useful. On the Palermo Stone the third row of year-boxes, dedicated to the reign of a king whose name is all but lost, may well be ascribed to Den. It is not possible to say how many years have been lost to the right but the second of the surviving boxes contains a reference to the 'Smiting of the Bedouins', which would nicely fit the description on the ivory label (compare figs. 64 and 66). Nor is it possible to estimate the total length of this king's reign since the row is broken to the left after fourteen recorded years. As the end of the king's name just appears to the extreme right and the royal name was apparently placed centrally over the row describing his achievements, this gives a minimum of twenty-eight years and more probably thirty-two for the length of this reign. Such are the uncertainties of dating even those Egyptian documents which are considered to be the most useful from a historical point of view.

Monuments erected to commemorate specific events are often more informative. The Annals of Thutmose III, recorded on the shrine he erected to Amen at Karnak, give a precise year-by-year record of the king's military campaigns as shown by these extracts:

> Year 31, first month of summer, day 3: List of that which His Majesty captured in this year
>
> Year 33: Behold, His Majesty was in the land of Retjenu. He set up a stela east of this water [the Euphrates], he set up another beside the stela of his father, the King of Upper and Lower Egypt, Aakheperure, Thutmose [I]

The events are are so vividly detailed that it is practically certain that they were transcribed from the official campaign diaries which Thutmose III had ordered to be kept. This is made clear in the introductory section of the Annals:

Behold, His Majesty commanded to be recorded the victories which he won from year 23 until year 42 when this inscription was recorded upon this sanctuary, that he might be given life forever. . . . Now all that His Majesty did, to this city or to that wretched foe and his army, was recorded each day by its name [i.e. date], recorded upon a roll of leather in the Temple of Amen unto this day.

In contrast, the original inscriptions on the huge obelisk which now stands in the square of St John Lateran in Rome, were carved towards the end of the reign of Thutmose III but later hieroglyphic texts added to the monument show that it was left to his grandson Thutmose IV to set it in its intended position, the forecourt before the Eighth Pylon in the temple of Karnak. Although this complicated history is inscribed upon the obelisk, it cannot be dated precisely because of the vague terms of the text.

Thutmose [IV] begotted of Re, beloved of Amen. It was His Majesty who beautified the single great obelisk being one which his father [sic] the King of Upper and Lower Egypt, Menkheperre, Thutmose [III] had brought [from the quarries of Aswan], after His Majesty had found this obelisk, it having spent thirty-five years lying upon its side in the hands of the craftsmen, on the south side of Karnak. [The memory of] my father demanded that I should erect it for him, I being his son, his saviour.

Another key to dating events within a reign came into play once the king had ruled for thirty years. This was traditionally the occasion of the king's Jubilee, the Heb Sed. After the first celebration in year 30, the king would celebrate a Jubilee every three or four years so that Ramesses II who ruled for nearly sixty-eight years is known to have celebrated thirteen and possibly fourteen Sed festivals. The occasion of any given Jubilee is a precise date, by Egyptian standards, as long as it it known when the first was celebrated. Hatshepsut erected obelisks to commemorate her first Jubilee, as is recorded at Deir el-Bahri, but she had a known reign of only twenty-two years. She dated her reign from a suspect claim to a co-regency with her father Thutmose I. Other monarchs are known to have dated their accession in this way, perhaps considering that elevation to the position of Crown Prince was a suitable point at which to start counting.

In order to celebrate Jubilees a record must have been kept of the date of accession of each monarch so that the years could be properly counted. At Medinet Habu, Ramesses III had inscribed a calendar of the festivals to be celebrated at his mortuary temple which, like Abydos, was to be considered as a national religious centre. The dedicatory inscription establishing these offerings starts with a date: 'Year 12, first month of summer, day 26, the day of the king's coronation upon the Horus Throne, when he received the regalia of his father Re.'

This indicates that the calendar of feasts was introduced on the anniversary of the king's coronation. It includes several new festivals to commemorate the king's victories like the 'Slaying of the Meshwesh' to be held in the first month of winter in memory of the king's second Libyan campaign. The Meshwesh were the principal Libyan tribe in the confederacy which attempted to invade Egypt in the eleventh year of the king's reign.

The calendar begins with the lists of offerings to be made on each day of the year as part of the daily temple ritual. There follow some of the monthly or half-monthly feasts then the great annual festivals are listed beginning with the anniversary of the coronation. The rest of the major feast days are given in chronological order starting with the 'Rising of Sirius' on New Year's Day and laying down how many days should be set aside for each celebration. In the case of the greatest Theban festival, that of Ipet, the holiday lasted for twenty-four days according to this calendar while during the reign of Thutmose III it was only eleven days long. In the Harris Papyrus the Ipet festival is said to have lasted for twenty-seven days showing that Ramesses III extended the celebration by three days in the later years of his reign. The offerings listed in the Harris Papyrus are even more extensive than the lavish requirements detailed in the

Medinet Habu calendar where the names of the treasuries, estates or religious establishments which were to be responsible for every offering are also given. This was a very precise administrative document as well as a calendar of religious observance.

King-lists such as that of Seti I at Abydos, or the Turin Canon, have limited value as far as absolute dating is concerned. Although several 'biographies' from private tombs record events during the lifetimes of their owners, these are rarely dated and even those dates which were included often give no more than the regnal year of a king who may or may not be named. The introduction to the *Story of Sinuhe*, a popular literary work of the Middle Kingdom, gives the date of the death of Amenemhet I: 'Year 30, third month of Inundation, day 7. The god mounted to his horizon, the King of Upper and Lower Egypt, Sehetepibre went up to heaven to be united with the sun's disc, the limbs of the god being merged with him who made him.'

Such precise dates are unusual. Even in the correspondence between Egypt and her subject territories or other independent kingdoms, dates are uncommon and letters have to be dated, or at least set in chronological order, by means of references to events and people and cross-referencing with the better-known chronologies of other civilizations. The later in the dynastic era that an event occurred, the more closely that event may be matched with a date in the Christian calendar since more external sources are available for cross-reference. During the Ptolemaic period, when there was continuous contact between the Egyptian court and Classical centres, official documents were usually kept in Greek and the months of the Egyptian calendar were given names which derived, in most cases, from the names of major religious festivals. In the hieroglyphic text on the Rosetta Stone, the traditional month-day-season dates are used with the occasional addition such as 'the day of the King's birthday'. There is little evidence otherwise to suggest that the Egyptians celebrated birthdays or kept account of age (fig.67).

Domestic matters were recorded on a day-to-day basis and the dates on documents such as the inventories of temple equipment and the records of deliveries to the storehouses show that the

67. A date taken from the Rosetta Stone.

Translation: Fourth month of summer, being the day of the birth of the Good God, Living Forever

Egyptian scribes dated their work as a regular practice. These dates may be quite detailed with the addition to the basic day, month and season, of a statement of the celebration of a religious festival. The 'Day Book' of the 'Scribe of the Tomb' at Deir el-Medina gives some useful historical information in between the very mundane details of the working practices of the 'Gang'.

When a new king came to the throne, the 'Gang' had a few days off, as at the accession of Ramesses-Siptah towards the end of the Nineteenth Dynasty. Then, after four days official holiday, the men's return to work was recorded by the Scribe as follows: 'They rejoiced and the Gang went to the Great Place in the first month of Winter, day 23, to work.' Also from the information in the 'Day Book', it seems that a 'week' of ten days was recognized with the ninth and tenth days being days of rest.

For the Workmen, deep in the cliff-cut tombs, artificial light was required. The Scribe also recorded deliveries of the materials used for making 'candles'. These were wicks of twisted linen placed in shallow bowls or saucers of oil to which salt had been added to prevent smoking. The linen used for these wicks was waste fabric, rags which were saved for the purpose, and the wick itself was such a commonplace object that it was used as the alphabetic hieroglyph representing an emphatic 'h'. The wicks were greased or 'annointed' with some kind of animal fat, a job carried out by the Workmen in the presence of representatives of the Village Elders, either the Foremen, their Deputies or the 'Guardians', since the fats and oils used for candle-making were all edible and therefore valuable. One hin jar of grease was expected to produce twenty candles while a large jar of oil for the saucers was enough to fuel

400 wicks, each of which was approximately 35 cm tall. Such careful standardization of the candle-lamps meant that each burned for a fairly predictable length of time.

The usual working day seems to have been divided into two four-hour shifts with a meal break at midday. The numbers of candles used by each 'side' of the 'Gang' during each shift were meticulously recorded by the Scribe. The following two entries from the 'Day Book' are dated to year 6 in the reign of Seti II.

> First month of Winter, day 5; consumption of candles made on that day:
>   right 6, left 6, total 12
>   right 6, left 5, total 11
> Fourth month of Inundation, day 16; consumption of candles made that day:
>   16 and 16, 32; 13 and 13, making 26; Total 58.

The two sets of numbers refer to the two 'sides' of the 'Gang' for the morning and afternoon shifts. Because of the valuable nature of the materials used for candles, a supply sufficient for only a few days was kept in the store-huts in the Valley of Kings at any one time. This explains the careful records which had to be kept as to the rate of use of these essential items. The varying numbers of candles used in one shift may be an indication of the length of time worked by each side, or the number of men working each four-hour session.

In later times, the Greek clepsydra or water-clock was introduced but for most of the Egyptian population the passage of time during the day was marked by the height of the sun just as the passing of the seasons was indicated by the height of the river. Only the bureaucrats found a need for a system which marked the passage of years. The Egyptians recognized a god of years, represented as a kneeling figure holding the palm-rib hieroglyph for 'year' in each hand. This is the figure who appears in the openwork carving

68. This Middle Kingdom stela bears a simple text which comprises, mainly, names and titles which may be found elsewhere in this book. A translation may be found on the following page but the reader may find it an interesting exercise to attempt a translation before turning the page.

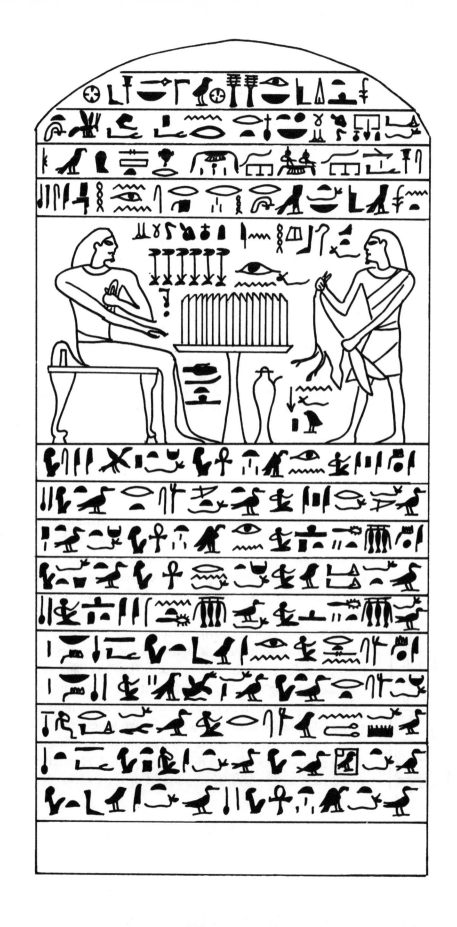

Translation (rows read right to left):

1. A boon which the king gives to Osiris, Lord of Djedu, the Great God, Lord of Abdu
2. That he might give an offering of bread and beer, oxen, fowl, alabaster and linen, and every good thing, to the Hereditary Prince, Nomarch, King's Seal-Bearer . . .
3. Sole Companion, Overseer of the Double House of Silver and Gold, Overseer of the Double House of Gold, Master of the Secrets
4. of the King in his every residence, Chancellor, Rehu-er-djer-sen, engendered of Hapy, justified (lit. True of Voice).
   Above table: 1000 each of bread, beer, ox, fowl, alabaster and linen
   Above figure on right: [Ritual] performed by the Lector Priest, Hekat-ef
   Between water jar and Hekat-ef: This is his brother
5. The venerable Ipi, born of Ankh-Mut; his wife, Pay-es;
6. His beloved son, Ipi; his beloved daughter, Sat-Usert, justified
7. The Venerable, Khenty-khety-hotep, born of Ankh-Mut; his wife, Sat-Pe
8. His daughter, Didiu; his wife, Ren-ef-ankh; his daughter, Henut;
9. His son, Khenty-khety-hotep; his son Khenty-khety-hotep, justified
10. The Venerable, Sen-Usert, born of Iubet, justified and venerated
11. His wife Sat-Usert; his son, Itjay, justified and venerated
12. His son, User-Montju; his son, Di-Sebek, justified
13. His daughter, Sat-Hathor; his daughter, Itep, justified
14. His daughter, Ankh-Mut, justified; his daughter Iubet

which decorates the back of the cedarwood chair from Tutankhamen's tomb. The god of years is also shown at the head of Table 15 which gives the various expressions used in Egyptian dates, and includes the names of some of the religious festivals. The numerals required for writing Egyptian dates will be found in the table at the end of Chapter 9 (page 171).

The 'God of Years', known as Heh, was symbolic of eternity and a similar figure with the year sign as a headdress, was used as the hieroglyph for the numeral 1,000,000. The Egyptians, at least the educated among the people of ancient times, comprehended such prolonged periods of time as one million years. The belief held above all others was that a man could live for eternity in the land of Osiris and the wish that a man's name should live forever was one of the most frequently and fervently repeated. Hieroglyphs conveyed such wishes with symbolic and pictorial elegance.

	year, regnal year			month
	day			New Year's Day (lit. opening the year)
	Season of Inundation			Season of Emergence (winter)
	Season of Drought (summer)			epagomenal days, (five added days)
	last day of month			morning
	star			night
	Sothis (Sirius) the Dog Star			The Morning Star (Venus)
	The Decans, stars marking hours			Imperishable Stars, (never setting)
	The Red Horus (Mars)			Horus, the Bull of Heaven (Saturn)
	Star of the Southern Sky (Jupiter)			New Moon Festival
	Wag Festival (18th day of 1st month)			Festival of the 18th day of the month
	Festival of Thoth (1st day of month)			Half Month Festival (15th day)
	Festival of Khoiakh, Festival of Osiris (5th month)			Festival of the Intoxication of Hathor (New Year)

Table 16: The Calendar

SELECT BIBLIOGRAPHY

BAINES John, and MALEK Jaromir *Atlas of Ancient Egypt* (London 1980)

BIERBRIER Morris *The Tomb-Builders of the Pharaohs* (London 1982)

GARDINER Sir Alan H *Egypt of the Pharaohs* (Oxford 1961)

GILLINGS Richard J *Mathematics in the Time of the Pharaohs* (New York 1982)

HART George *A Dictionary of Egyptian Gods and Goddesses* (London 1986)

HART George *Pharaohs and Pyramids* (London 1991)

HART George *Egyptian Myths* (London 1992)

JAMES T G H *Pharaoh's People* (London 1984)

JANSSEN Rosalind and Jac *Growing up in Ancient Egypt* (London 1990)

KEMP Barry *Ancient Egypt: Anatomy of a Civilization* (London 1989)

KITCHEN Kenneth A *Pharaoh Triumphant: the Life and Times of Ramesses II* (Warminster 1982)

KOLOS Daniel, and ASSAAD Hany *The Name of the Dead: Tutankhamun Translated* (Ontario 1979)

LURKER Manfred *The Gods and Symbols of Ancient Egypt* (London 1980)

MANNICHE Lise *City of the Dead: Thebes in Egypt* (London 1987)

MARTIN Geoffrey T *The Hidden Tombs of Memphis* (London 1991)

MURNANE William J *United With Eternity: A Concise Guide to the Monuments of Medinet Habu* (Chicago 1980)

PARKINSON R B *Voices From Ancient Egypt* (London 1991)

QUIRKE Stephen *Who Were the Pharaohs?* (London 1990)

REEVES Nicholas *The Complete Tutankhamun* (London 1990)

RICE Michael *Egypt's Making* (London 1990)

ROMER John *Valley of the Kings* (London 1981)

ROSE John *The Sons of Re: Cartouches of the Kings of Egypt* (Warrington 1985)

WATTERSON Barbara *The Gods of Ancient Egypt* (London 1984)

WATTERSON Barbara *Women in Ancient Egypt* (Stroud 1991)

WHALE Sheila *The Family in the Eighteenth Dynasty of Egypt* (Sydney 1989)

INDEX